SCIENCE **SCOPE**
CHEMISTRY

Frank Benfield

Hodder & Stoughton

A MEMBER OF THE HODDER HEADLINE GROUP

Contents

Preface

Chemistry is a challenging subject; many of its concepts and ideas relate to the invisible and we rely heavily on models to understand them. However, the study of it is very rewarding and worthwhile, not least because of the excitement of being involved in the branch of science which has had, and continues to have, the greatest impact on our technological society.

I have sought to emphasise the important part that chemistry plays in our everyday lives; for example in providing new materials, developing cleaner and lasting energy resources, in monitoring and reducing pollution and in understanding the changing Earth on which we live.

This book covers the material for pupils in Years 7, 8 and 9 following the Materials and their properties section of the Key Stage 3 Science National Curriculum or the Common Entrance Examination at 13+ Science Syllabus (Chemistry).

Particular attention has been paid to the inclusion of extension material, which will aid pupils of average and above average abilities, who are aiming for a high level of achievement. There has been a conscious effort to offer opportunities to allow the most able pupils to display and develop their powers of reasoning, synthesis and analysis, particularly in respect of experimental information.

The following features have been included in the book:

* Test Yourself Questions to consolidate and reinforce understanding.
* Extension Boxes, which contain material aimed specifically at those pupils aiming for the higher tiers or following the Common Entrance examination.
* Ideas and Evidence boxes that highlight the work of notable scientists or emphasise significant advances in chemistry.
* Summaries bringing together all the ideas in the chapter.
* End-of-Chapter Questions to draw together the ideas of the chapter and to encourage students to appreciate the links between them.

Acknowledgements

I should like to thank Lis Tribe and Kate Fowler at Hodder and Stoughton for their sound editorial advice and judgement.

Frank Benfield

Matching Grid

	National Curriculum Programme of Study	Key Stage 3 Scheme of Work	Common Entrance Examination Syllabus
Chapter 1 States of matter	7G	1a, 1b, 2a	1a, 1b, 2c
Chapter 2 Chemical reactions	7F	1e, 1f, 1g, 2h	1e
Chapter 3 Reactions of acids and alkalis	7E	3d, 3e, 3f, 3g, 3h	3d, 3e,
Chapter 4 Solutions	7H	1g, 1h, 2a, 2b	1h, 2a, 2b
Chapter 5 Atoms, elements and compounds	8E	1c, 1d, 1e	1b, 1c, 1d, 1f
Chapter 6 Compounds and mixtures	8F	1e, 1g	1b, 1e, 1g
Chapter 7 Rocks and weathering	8G	2d, 2e, 2f	2d
Chapter 8 The rock cycle	8H	2d, 2e, 2f	2e, 2f
Chapter 9 Reactions of metals and metal compounds	9E	3a	3a, 3e, 3f
Chapter 10 Patterns of reactivity	9F	3b, 3c	3b, 3c
Chapter 11 Environmental chemistry	9G	3i	3g, 3i
Chapter 12 Using chemistry	9H	2g, 2i	3g, 3h

1 The states of matter

Everything around us is either a gas, a liquid or a solid. Solids, liquids and gases are the three **states of matter**. The picture shows some of the solids, liquids and gases around us.

We can tell what state of matter something is by the way that it behaves. You can pour a can of cola into a glass and it takes up the shape of the glass, but the volume of cola will not change – it will not expand to fill two glasses. The glass always looks the same: solids have a fixed shape. Gases completely fill the space they occupy: you can smell the cooking from your kitchen all over the house.

State of matter	Shape	Volume
gas	not fixed	not fixed
liquid	not fixed	fixed
solid	fixed	fixed

Table 1 ▲   Summary of the states of matter for gases, liquids and gases.

Test Yourself

1   What are the three states of matter?

2   Identify two examples of each state of matter in your classroom.

3   Which state of matter has:
   a) a fixed shape and a fixed volume
   b) no fixed shape but a fixed volume?

The particle model of solids, liquids and gases

Scientists use **models** to help them to understand tricky concepts, so models are often used when very small particles, such as atoms and molecules, are involved.

We cannot see exactly how the atoms or molecules in solids, liquids and gases are actually arranged because they are too small. So scientists use a model to explain the differences between solids, liquids and gases. This is called the particle model of solids, liquids and gases. It is based on the facts that:

- All substances are made of tiny, moving particles which are invisible to the naked eye.
- The particles are moving all the time. On average particles move faster the higher the temperature.

We try to understand how the three states of matter behave by imagining that they contain particles that are big enough to see. In our models the particles are billions of times bigger than the real particles.

We know how large amounts of gases, liquids and solids behave, but the particle model tries to go further than this. It tries to explain their properties in terms of the way their particles move and are arranged in terms of how strong the forces are between the particles (Table 2).

State of matter	Forces between particles	How freely can the particles move?	How far apart are the particles?	Model
Gas	very weak	very freely – move quickly	very far apart	
Liquid	weak	freely – move less quickly than gas particles	fairly close together	
Solid	strong	do not move from place to place, just vibrate	touching each other	

Table 2 ▲   The three states of matter

In solids, the particles are packed closely together in a regular pattern. This explains why they have a fixed shape and a fixed volume. In all states of matter the particles are in a constant state of motion, but in solids they can only vibrate from side to side.

In a gas, the particles are not held together and so they move freely from place to place. This is why gases spread out to fill the container they are in. Gases do not have a fixed shape or a fixed volume.

The particles in a liquid are able to move at random like those in a gas, but are much closer together. In liquids, the particles can roll around each other. So, a liquid has a fixed volume but will take the shape of its container.

Test Yourself

4   In which state of matter are the particles:
    a) furthest apart
    b) closest together?

5   In which states of matter can particles move from place to place?

6   How are the arrangements of the particles in a gas and a liquid:
    a) similar
    b) different?

Compressing things

Compressing gases

There is a lot of space between the particles in a gas so they can be pushed closer together quite easily. Scientists say that it is easy to **compress** a gas. Because a gas always fills all the space available, it springs back again if the force compressing it is removed. The ability of a gas to spring back again is put to use in pneumatic tyres. When the tyres on your bike are properly inflated, the air in them absorbs the shocks when you go over bumps in the road. Instead of you feeling the shock, the gas in the tyre is compressed; the gas then springs back when you are over the bump.

Figure 2 shows that if the volume of a gas is reduced, its pressure increases because the gas particles hit the walls of the container more often.

a)
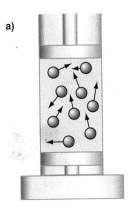

b)
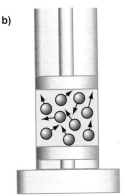

Figure 2 ▲   Gases can be compressed

Test Yourself

7 Jodi squeezes a tennis ball in her hand.
  a) What happens to the air inside it when she does this?
  b) Explain what will happen when she lets the tennis ball go.

8 Jodi then tries to change the shape of a snooker ball by squeezing it. Explain why she cannot do it.

9 Explain in your own words why a gas exerts a pressure.

10 Why does a gas exert more pressure if its volume is reduced?

Can liquids and solids be compressed?

Some expensive mountain bikes have hydraulic brakes. A liquid carries the force put on the brake lever to the brake pads. Hydraulic brakes work because the liquid cannot be compressed. All of the force from the brake lever goes to the brakes.

The pipe that carries the liquid is flexible. This shows that a liquid can take up any shape; the pipe changes shape when the bike is being ridden. A liquid has a fixed volume so the particles cannot be forced any closer together. If the liquid could be compressed, all you would do when you put the brakes on would be to reduce the volume of the liquid, without applying the brakes!

The solid parts of the brake system, such as the brake lever, cylinders and brake pads, cannot be compressed. Come to that, the bike itself is made of solid metal – just imagine the result if the metal could be compressed!

Test Yourself

11 a) Explain in your own words how a hydraulic brake works.
  b) Why would it be dangerous if air got into the liquid used in the brakes?

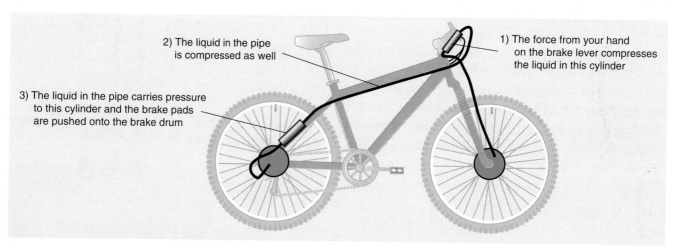

2) The liquid in the pipe is compressed as well

1) The force from your hand on the brake lever compresses the liquid in this cylinder

3) The liquid in the pipe carries pressure to this cylinder and the brake pads are pushed onto the brake drum

Figure 3 ▲ The hydraulic brakes of a mountain bike work because liquids cannot be compressed.

Changes of state

A lump of ice in a glass of cola soon melts, turning solid ice into liquid water. The reverse happens when liquid water from the tap is left in the freezer overnight. Liquid water in a kettle turns to steam when it boils and then turns to liquid water again when it reaches the cold glass in the kitchen window.

Figure 4 ▲   What would life be like if solids could be compressed?

Melting, freezing, boiling, condensing, and subliming are called **changes of state**. The changes of state are summarised in Figure 6.

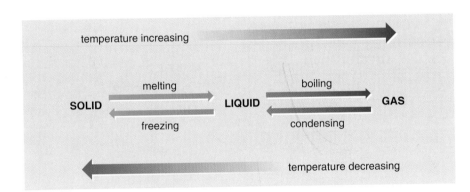

Figure 6 ▲   Changes of state

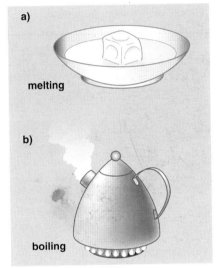

Figure 5 ▲   a) melting and b) boiling

- **Melting** – Heating a solid makes the particles vibrate more and more violently. The forces holding the particles in place are overcome and can no longer hold them in a regular pattern, so the solid melts to form a liquid.
- **Boiling** – Heating a liquid causes the particles to vibrate even more violently and move even more quickly. If the temperature is high enough they can escape the attractive forces of the neighbouring particles and form a gas.
- **Condensation** – Cooling a gas slows the particles down so that the attractive forces between the particles are able to pull them together sufficiently to allow a liquid to form.
- **Freezing** – Cooling a liquid reduces the motion of the particles even more. The forces between the particles are now strong enough to hold them in a regular pattern to form a solid.
- **Sublimation** – A few substances can go straight from a solid to a gas without melting. This is called sublimation. Iodine and solid carbon dioxide are two substances that do this.

In the laboratory, some chemicals are solids such as zinc, some are liquids such as mercury, and some are gases such as hydrogen. This is because the temperature at which each chemical melts, or turns into a gas (boils) is different. The temperature at which a chemical melts is called its melting point. The temperature at which a chemical turns into a gas is called its boiling point.

A chemical kept at a temperature below its melting point is a solid but it will be a liquid when the temperature is above its melting point. If the temperature is even higher, the liquid will boil to become a gas.

'Room temperature' is a vague term, but it is taken to be about 25 °C for most purposes. Water is a liquid at room temperature. At 25 °C it is above its melting point but below its boiling point.

Table 3 shows how the melting and boiling points of a substance affect whether the substance will be a solid, a liquid or a gas at room temperature.

State of matter	Melting point	Boiling point
solid	greater than 25 °C	greater than 25 °C
liquid	less than 25 °C	greater than 25 °C
gas	less than 25 °C	less than 25 °C

Table 3 ▲

Test Yourself

12 The table shows the boiling and melting points of some substances.

Substance	Melting point (°C)	Boiling point (°C)
A	98	892
B	−7	58
C	−182	−162
D	650	1110
E	18	286
F	−78	−33

At room temperature, which substances will be:
a) liquids
b) solids
c) gases?

Extension box

In the particle model of gases and liquids we have assumed that all the particles move at the same speed and that all of them move more quickly as the temperature increases. Since we know that the particles constantly collide with one another this assumption must be incorrect. Collisions will cause some particles to slow down or some particles to speed up, as well as changing their direction of movement.

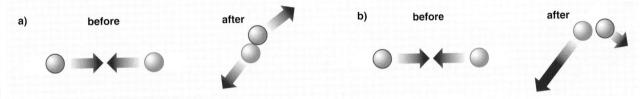

Figure 7 ▲ a) Collision slows down both particles b) Faster particle slows down, slower particle speeds up

In fact, the particles have a whole range of energies, in the same way as people walking down a busy street will be moving at different speeds as they jostle into each other. The *average* energy of the particles increases as the temperature increases but the energies of individual particles can still be very different. Increasing the temperature does not increase the energy of every particle but increases the average energy of all of them.

This helps us to understand why liquids evaporate more quickly as the temperature increases. The particles in a liquid have a whole range of energies but only those with the most energy can escape the attractions of the other particles in the liquid to become a gas. Raising the temperature gives more particles enough energy to overcome the attractions of their neighbours and so more particles escape.

Be careful to distinguish between boiling and **evaporation**. Boiling occurs at a fixed temperature (100 °C for water); evaporation occurs at all temperatures, but more rapidly as the temperature rises.

Test Yourself

13 What is a 'change of state'?

14 What changes of state take place when:
   a) steam reaches a cold window
   b) butter is put into a hot saucepan
   c) a candle is lit
   d) petrol is spilt on a garage forecourt?

Temperature changes during boiling

James bet Kate that he could heat water to a higher temperature than she could. They each took a beaker with the same amount of water in it and started heating. James used two Bunsen burners to heat his beaker, Kate used one. They each measured the temperature of their water every minute. Their results are shown in the graph in Figure 8.

A liquid cannot be heated above its boiling point. Any extra heat supplied just makes the particles escape from the liquid more quickly.

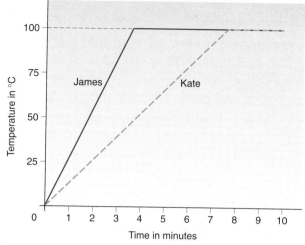

Figure 8 ▲

It is the liquid particles with the most energy that can escape the liquid and evaporate. It is the liquid particles with less energy that remain. This cools the liquid that remains, so its temperature will fall. We use this process to cool ourselves during exercise. The liquid used is our sweat.

Figure 9 ▲ Evaporation of perspiration cools an athlete

Temperature changes during melting

Heating a solid increases its temperature and makes its particles vibrate faster. During melting, the heat energy goes into making the particles in the solid break out of their regular arrangement to become a liquid, but has no effect on the temperature. Figure 10 shows how the temperature changes when a solid is heated.

Figure 10 ▶

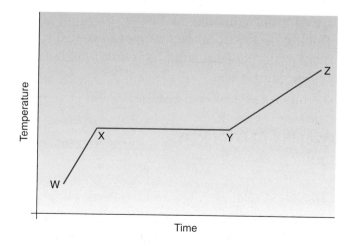

Use Figure 10 to help you answer these questions.

19 What is happening to the particles between W and X? Why is this happening?

20 Which part of the graph represents:
a) a solid
b) a liquid?

21 What states of matter would you see in the part of the graph between X and Y?

22 Mark on the temperature axis the melting point of the substance.

23 Explain why the temperature does not change from X to Y.

The movement of particles

Brownian motion

A Scottish botanist, called Robert Brown (1773–1858) was the first person to prove that particles are moving about rapidly. Brown was looking through his microscope at very small pollen grains suspended in water and he noticed that they were moving around in a haphazard way. The typical path followed by one of the grains is shown in Figure 11. He named the phenomenon 'Brownian motion'.

Brownian motion can be explained as follows. The suspended pollen grain is constantly and randomly bombarded from all sides by particles of the liquid. If the pollen grain is very small, the hits it takes at one instant in time from one side may be stronger than the hits from other sides, causing it to jump.

These small random jumps are what make up Brownian motion.

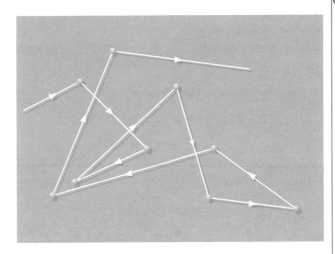

Figure 11 ▲ Brownian motion

The mixing of gases

An inflated balloon goes down after a few days, even though there seem to be no holes in the balloon. The tiny gas particles are moving rapidly and randomly inside the balloon. Sooner or later the gas particles escape through holes in the balloon much bigger than they are, but still too small for us to see.

Gases with low densities like helium, leak faster than denser gases, such as air. Helium balloons seen at fairgrounds have a metal coating to help reduce leaks. The particles of helium gas move much faster than those of air at the same temperature. The helium particles are therefore more likely to find a hole in the balloon more quickly. Helium leaks out of a rubber balloon in a few minutes, see Figure 12.

The particle model also explains why gases spontaneously mix with each other. If a gas jar of air is placed on top of another gas jar containing orange bromine vapour, the two gases quickly mix. This happens even though the bromine vapour is denser than air, and might be expected to stay in the lower gas jar, see Figure 13.

This spontaneous mixing of gases is called **diffusion**. It happens because of the rapid random motion of the particles in each gas.

Diffusion also occurs in liquids. This is why, if you add a small amount of blackcurrant juice to a glass of water, the colour eventually spreads throughout the glass, see Figure 14.

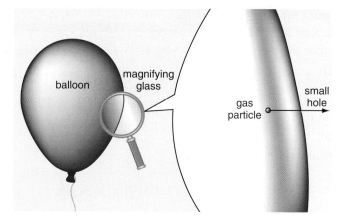

Figure 12 ▲

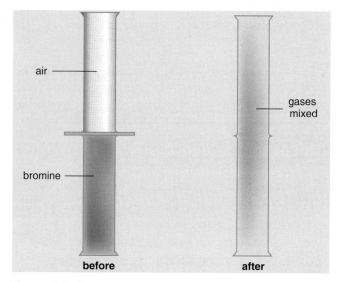

Figure 13 ▲

Test Yourself

24 What is 'diffusion'?

25 Explain why some gases diffuse more quickly than others.

26 Explain why gases diffuse faster than liquids.

Density: how tightly packed are the particles?

We know from everyday life that the same volume of different substances can weigh different amounts. A full suitcase weighs more than an empty one – clothes are heavier than air. An empty bottle of cola weighs less than a full one – cola is also heavier that air.

Figure 14 ▲

You can find the mass of something by weighing it. The bigger the **mass** of something the more it weighs. Laboratory balances record masses in grams or kilograms. The mass of something measures the amount of material in it. Scientists use the idea of **density** to compare the masses of the same volume of different substances.

The cola bottle with air inside weighs 40.0 g. If we pump all the air out of the cola bottle it weighs only 38.7 g. So, the air in the one litre bottle weighs 1.3 g (40.0 g – 38.7 g).

Figure 15 ▲ A litre of air weighs much less than a litre of cola

We can work out the density of a substance using the formula:

$$\text{density} = \frac{\text{mass}}{\text{volume}}$$

A litre of air has a mass of 1.3 g, so its density is $\dfrac{1.3}{1} = 1.3$ g/litre.

A litre of cola has a mass of 1000 g, so its density is $\dfrac{1000}{1} = 1000$ g/litre.

A litre is 1000 cm³, so these densities can be expressed in g/cm³ (see Table 5).

Substance	Density in g/litre	Density in g/cm³
Air (a gas)	1.3	0.0013
Cola (a liquid)	1000	1.0
Iron (a solid)	7900	7.9

Table 5 ▲

The density of iron has been added to the table. Note the very high value. The particles in solids are tightly packed together compared to liquids, so solids are denser. Gases are not very dense because the particles are very far apart: there aren't many gas particles in a given volume compared to the other states of matter.

Test Yourself

27 Work out the densities of the substances in the diagrams.

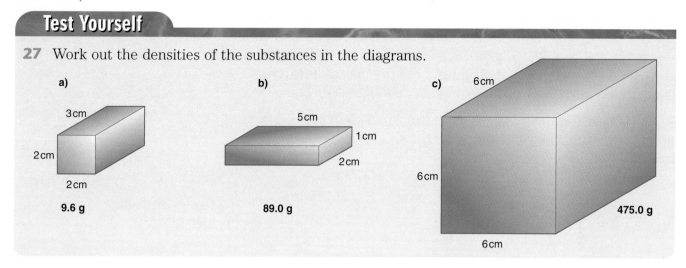

a)

3 cm

2 cm

2 cm

9.6 g

b)

5 cm

1 cm

2 cm

89.0 g

c)

6 cm

6 cm

6 cm

475.0 g

Heating particles

Most substances **expand** when they are heated. Heating gases and liquids makes the particles move more violently, so they occupy a bigger volume. If a gas or liquid is heated in a closed container where it cannot expand, the pressure of the expanding gas may burst the container.

When solids are heated the particles in them vibrate more violently and take up more room, so the solid expands. Railway lines have gaps in them to allow for expansion. Without these gaps the rails would buckle on hot days, see Figure 16.

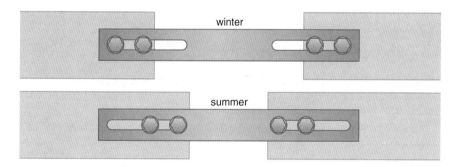

winter

summer

Figure 16 ▲

Expansion and **contraction** can be useful. The iron hoops on wagon wheels were fitted by heating them so they expanded. The hot hoop was then placed over the wooden wheel and quickly cooled with water to shrink it again. The hoop was then held firmly in place.

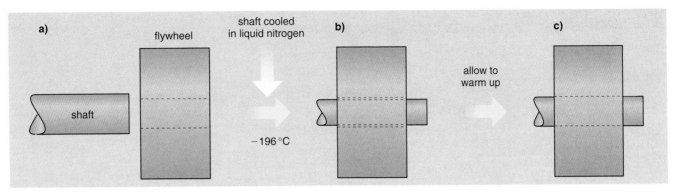

Figure 17 ▲ Shrink fitting: a) shaft will not fit through flywheel at room temperature; b) shaft shrinks and now fits; c) shaft expands on warming back to room temperature and is now a tight fit in the flywheel

Most substances contract when they are cooled. Contraction is used by engineers in a process, called 'shrink fitting'. Engineers use liquid nitrogen at −196 °C to do the cooling. When an item is cooled it shrinks and so will fit easily into a hole. When the cooled item warms up again, the fit in the hole is very tight. Figure 17 explains how shrink fitting works.

Evaluating the particle model

A model is judged good or bad depending on how well it helps to explain observed facts. Table 6 shows some properties of gases, liquids and solids, together with how these properties are explained according to the particle model. The particle model explains quite well how the three states of matter behave and so it is a good model.

Observation	Explanation in terms of the particle theory
Gas pressure	The particles in the gas hit the walls of the container, creating the pressure
Diffusion of gases and liquids	The random motion of the particles ensures that the particles intermingle
Liquids and solids cannot be compressed	Their particles are packed close together, making it very difficult to push them any closer together
Melting and boiling	Heating gives the particles more energy until eventually they can overcome the forces holding them together in the solid or liquid
Expansion on heating	The particles move more violently when heated so they jostle into each other more, and are forced apart

Table 6 ▲

Test Yourself

28 What do scientists mean by the word 'model'?

29 What is meant by a 'good model'?

30 Explain whether or not the particle model is a good model for what goes on in the playground at school during break. You should think about how the people in the playground are arranged and how they are moving.

Summary

✔ The three states of matter are solid, liquid and gas.

✔ Solids, liquids and gases are made of individual particles.

✔ Scientists use models to help explain difficult ideas.

✔ The particles in gases and liquids are in constant random motion.

✔ The particles in gases diffuse to fill all the available space with the gas.

✔ In solids the particles can only vibrate, but they can't move about.

✔ Gases can be compressed, but solids and liquids can't be compressed.

✔ The three states of matter can be brought about by heating or cooling.

✔ The density of a substance is the mass of a cubic centimetre of the substance.

End-of-Chapter Questions

1 Explain in your own words the following key terms you have met in this chapter:

states of matter

model

compress

change of state

melting

boiling

condensation

freezing

sublimation

evaporation

pressure

diffusion

mass

density

2 Use the particle theory to explain the following.

a) A bicycle tyre that has been inflated until it feels hard on a hot summer's day feels softer in the evening.

b) Someone spills some petrol on a garage forecourt when filling their car. The smell of petrol can be detected a long way from where petrol was spilt.

c) A metal screw top which has become stuck on a glass jar can often be loosened by running it under hot water.

d) A glass of water with ice cubes in it stays at 0 °C until the last of the ice has melted.

End-of-Chapter Questions continued

3 The diagram shows the three states of matter and how they can be converted from one to the other.

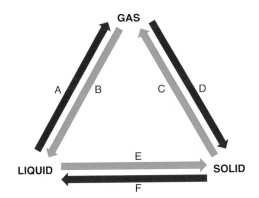

a) Name the changes represented by the letters A to F.

b) i) Name a substance that undergoes change F at 0 °C.

   ii) At what temperature does this substance undergo change A?

c) Name a substance that can undergo change C.

d) Which of the changes A to F require heat energy to make them take place?

e) Draw diagrams to show the arrangement of the particles:

   i) before and after change A

   ii) before and after change F.

4 Ammonia vapour reacts with hydrochloric acid vapour to form a white mist. The diagram shows an experiment in which this is happening.

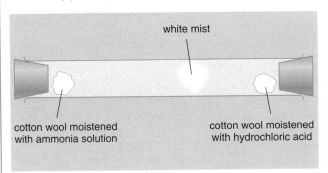

white mist

cotton wool moistened with ammonia solution

cotton wool moistened with hydrochloric acid

a) The white mist did not form for a minute or two after the experiment was set up. Explain why.

b) Which vapour diffused more quickly, ammonia or hydrochloric acid? Explain your answer.

c) What change could you make to the experiment to make the white mist form more quickly? Explain why the change you suggest would have this effect.

5 John devised an experiment to show how the particles in a gas diffuse. His apparatus is shown in the diagram. It is a shallow tray divided by a partition with a hole in it. He used marbles to represent the particles. John shook the tray from side to side to make the marbles move.

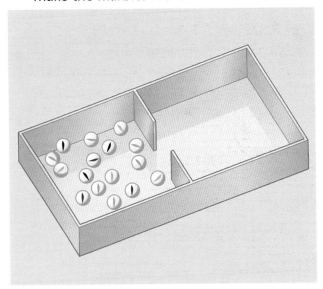

a) In what ways is John's experiment:

   i) similar to a real gas

   ii) different from a real gas?

b) i) The faster John shakes the tray the faster the marbles find their way into side B of his tray. Explain why this happens.

   ii) What would you do to a real gas to bring about a similar change?

2 Chemical reactions

C hemical reactions are happening around us all the time. Some are more spectacular than others. Fireworks exploding into bursts of coloured light and explosives tearing through a mine or quarry are two very loud and very obvious examples of chemical reactions. Other reactions happen much more slowly, such as the baking of a cake or the rusting of a car. Although these examples seem very different, they all share something in common. In all of the examples given, the starting materials, or reactants, are being changed permanently into different materials, called products. This chapter will explore more closely what happens when substances react together.

Colourful and noisy – a spectacular chemical reaction

In chemistry, when we talk about chemical reactions, we use word equations to help us see what has happened. Word equations always have the **reactants**, the substances we start with, on the left. The **products**, the substances which are formed, go on the right. We separate the two with an arrow.

An example of a word equation is shown below for the reaction between sodium and chlorine:

sodium + chlorine → sodium chloride
      reactants   product

When we have more than one reactant or product, we write the equation as:

reactant W + reactant X → product Y + product Z

For example:

magnesium + hydrochloric acid → magnesium chloride + hydrogen

zinc + sulphuric acid → zinc sulphate + hydrogen

How do we know when a reaction has taken place?

Changes in appearance

One of the easiest ways of spotting that a chemical reaction has taken place is that the reactants look different from the products. You can see this when you make a cake. The finished cake looks completely different from the ingredients you started with.

Table 1 lists some reactions that are obvious because the reactants look different from the products.

Reactants	Products
sodium (silvery metal) and chlorine (green gas)	sodium chloride (white solid)
hydrogen (colourless gas) and oxygen (colourless gas)	water (colourless liquid)
magnesium (silvery metal) and oxygen (colourless gas)	magnesium oxide (white solid)
copper carbonate (green solid), when heated	copper oxide (black solid) and carbon dioxide (colourless gas)
copper carbonate (green solid) and sulphuric acid (colourless liquid)	copper sulphate (blue solution) and carbon dioxide (colourless gas) and water (colourless liquid)
zinc (silvery metal) and hydrochloric acid (colourless liquid)	zinc chloride (colourless solution) and hydrogen (colourless gas)

Table 1 ▲

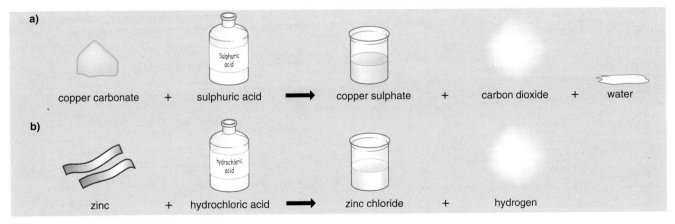

Figure 1 ▲ Products of chemical reactions often look different from the reactants

Test Yourself

1   When a chemical reaction happens, new products are formed which are completely different from the original reactants. We have given the example of baking a cake. Can you think of any other examples of chemical reactions happening in the kitchen?

2   Use Table 1 to help you complete word equations for following reactions:
   a) sodium + oxygen →
   b) zinc + oxygen →
   c) magnesium + chlorine →
   d) magnesium + hydrochloric acid →
   e) sodium carbonate + sulphuric acid →
   f) copper carbonate + hydrochloric acid →

Energy changes

All chemical reactions involve energy changes, usually in the form of heat energy, light or sound, and sometimes all three. You may be able to think of examples from everyday life.

Heat energy is the most useful form of energy we can get from chemical reactions, because heat can then be changed into other forms of energy. Some of the most violent chemical reactions involve explosions and these make a lot of noise as well as releasing heat and producing flames.

Figure 2 ▲   a) Burning methane releases heat energy.
b) Burning the iron filings on a sparkler releases light energy.
c) Burning gunpowder releases sound energy.

The formation of gases

If you can see a gas being produced, you can be sure that a chemical reaction is taking place.

Formation of hydrogen

A gas is given off in reactions between acids and reactive metals. This gas is hydrogen. The general equation for the chemical reaction is:

acid + reactive metal → metal salt + hydrogen

Zinc, iron and magnesium are reactive metals. They all react with acids to give hydrogen.

hydrochloric acid + zinc → zinc chloride + hydrogen

Testing for hydrogen

It is easy to see when a reaction has taken place between a metal and an acid. This is because the metal goes into the solution. However, we still need to test the gas to show that it is hydrogen.

Hydrogen burns very easily; it is said to be **flammable**. The test for hydrogen is to apply a match to the mouth of a test tube of the gas. If the gas burns with a squeaky 'pop' then it is hydrogen.

Other flammable gases, such as natural gas, make no sound when they burn. Hydrogen burns much more quickly than other gases and the 'pop' is caused by the flame moving quickly down the test tube. Other gases burn too slowly to make any sound.

Figure 3 ▲ Testing for hydrogen

Formation of carbon dioxide

All metal carbonates react with acids to give a salt of the acid, carbon dioxide and water. The general equation for the reaction is:

acid + metal carbonate → metal salt + carbon dioxide + water

hydrochloric + magnesium → magnesium + carbon + water
acid   carbonate   carbonate   dioxide

Testing for carbon dioxide

One way of showing that a metal carbonate has reacted with an acid would be to test the gas produced to show that it is carbon dioxide. Limewater (a solution of calcium hydroxide) turns cloudy when carbon dioxide is passed into it. Figure 4 shows how to test for carbon dioxide.

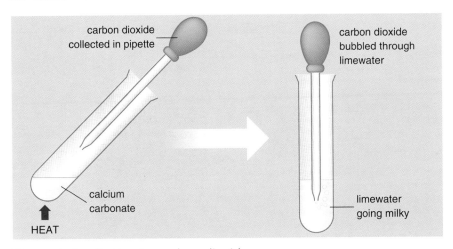

Figure 4 ▲ Testing for carbon dioxide

The cloudiness in the solution is caused by a **precipitate** of solid calcium carbonate that does not dissolve in water.

calcium hydroxide + carbon dioxide → calcium carbonate + water
(in solution)   (gas)   (solid)   (liquid)

Test Yourself

3 Complete the word equation:
   reactive metal + acid → ____ + ____

4 Find out about a use for copper that depends on its lack of reactivity with water.
   What would happen to iron if you used it instead of copper for this use?

5 Describe the test for hydrogen and explain why it works.

6 List two ways you could use to tell that a reaction has taken place when zinc and sulphuric acid are mixed.

7 Complete the word equations for the following reactions:
   a) metal carbonate + acid → ____ + ____ + ____

8 Describe the test for carbon dioxide and write a word equation for it.

Chemical reactions occurring around us

Corrosion

Metals react with acids in the environment. When metals react with acids, they dissolve away. This is called **corrosion**. All metals, except the least reactive ones, such as silver and gold, corrode to some extent. Iron corrodes easily – the process is called rusting. A huge amount of money is spent trying to prevent rusting and in replacing iron articles (such as cars) which have been damaged by rusting. Copper corrodes very slowly compared to iron, but eventually becomes covered with a green coating of copper compounds.

a)

b)
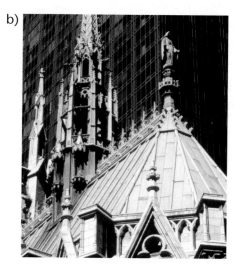

Figure 5 ▲ Corrosion of iron a) and copper b)

Burning (combustion)

One of the first chemical reactions that humans will have seen must have been burning – for example when lightning strikes a tree. Early humans used the heat energy and light energy, which was produced by burning, for all sorts of things:

- to cook with,
- to keep warm,
- to heat up metals to shape them.

The substances which we use to burn are called fuels.

Scientists have tried to explain what happens when substances burn.

Test Yourself

9 What is meant by *corrosion*? Explain why corrosion is a problem.

10 Explain why heat energy is so useful.

Ideas and Evidence

The phlogiston theory of burning

When anything burns, heat is given out. But what happens to the substance which is burnt?

The first attempt to explain burning was the phlogiston (pronounced *flojiston*) theory. This theory led to some scientific problems.

The term 'phlogiston' was first used in the early eighteenth century by the German scientist Stahl. The main ideas of the phlogiston theory were:

1 All substances contain phlogiston and a residue; the residue was known as 'calx'.
2 When substances burn they lose their phlogiston.

A word equation to explain the burning of magnesium using the phlogiston theory might be:

$$\text{magnesium} \rightarrow \text{calx} + \text{phlogiston} + \text{heat}$$

The phlogiston was lost to the air and we would now recognise the 'calx' as magnesium oxide.

Any reaction with the air was explained by the theory, even the rusting of iron.

$$\text{iron} \rightarrow \text{calx} + \text{phlogiston} + \text{heat}$$
$$\text{(rust)}$$

Notice that phlogiston and heat are not the same – phlogiston was thought to be a substance.

Some substances, such as carbon and sulphur, were thought to be almost pure phlogiston because they leave little or no calx when they are burnt. At that time there was no way to weigh the oxides of carbon and sulphur, which are gases.

Ideas and Evidence   continued

The phlogiston theory seemed to explain some chemical observations.

1   Substances like coal and wood lose weight when they burn because they lose phlogiston.
2   Carbon could turn a calx back to the metal again by giving up its phlogiston to the calx.

$$carbon + calx \rightarrow metal$$
(nearly pure
phlogiston)

But there were serious difficulties with the theory:

★   Magnesium (and other metals) formed a calx which weighed MORE than the magnesium.
★   Sulphur (and other non-metals) formed a calx which weighed LESS than the sulphur.

This meant that the phlogiston in metals had negative weight, but the phlogiston in non-metals had positive weight!

The test of any good scientific theory is that it should allow predictions to be made, which can then be tested by doing experiments. The phlogiston theory failed this test miserably. The theory was soon discarded as incorrect, following the work of the French chemist, Antoine Lavoisier (1743–1794).

Lavoisier realised that a metal increased in mass when it was burned because it had reacted with air. However, he did not know which substance in the air the metal had reacted with. The vital clue came with the discovery of oxygen by the English chemist Joseph Priestley in 1774.

Lavoisier did some experiments to show that metals reacted with the oxygen in the air. These experiments, and the apparatus he used, are described here.

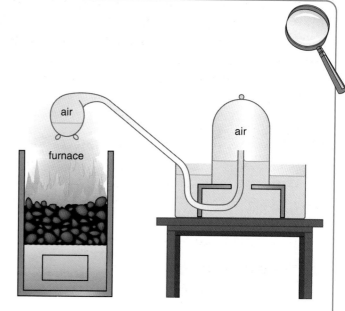

Figure 6 ▲   Lavoisier's apparatus

Lavoisier's experiment involved mercury in a retort. The retort had a long neck that lead to some air trapped in a bell jar by another quantity of mercury. He marked the mercury level in the bell jar at the start of the experiment and then heated the retort. Soon a red solid started to collect on the surface of the mercury in the retort, but after a while no more red solid was formed.

Lavoisier let the apparatus cool and worked out that about one fifth of the air in the apparatus had disappeared. The gas that remained did not support combustion or life. Lavoisier named the gas *azote* in French – we now know this gas as nitrogen.

Lavoisier collected the red solid from the retort and heated it. The red solid decomposed to give exactly the same volume of oxygen as had disappeared from the air. He mixed the nitrogen with this oxygen and found that the resulting 'air' behaved very much as the air in the rest of his laboratory did.

Lavoisier's work showed that burning involved only the oxygen in the air. When things burn, they combine with the oxygen to form oxides. The oxides formed always weigh more than the substances that were burnt.

A simple experiment to show that oxygen is needed for things to burn is shown in Figure 7. The water rises up the jar as the candle burns. The candle burns until all the oxygen in the air has been used and then it goes out. The water rises one-fifth of the way up the jar because one-fifth of the air is oxygen, the rest is mostly nitrogen.

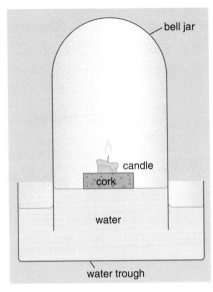

Figure 7 ▲

Test Yourself

11 An experiment like the one shown in Figure 7 was carried out and the candle burned for 2 minutes before going out. Explain the effect on the time the candle burns of using:
a) a smaller bell jar
b) a bigger candle.

12 When the burning candle under the bell jar went out there was still gas left in the bell jar. Explain why.

Using the apparatus in Figure 8, we can find out what is formed as the candle burns. Air is drawn over the candle and the substances formed pass into the test tubes. The anhydrous copper sulphate turns from white to blue, showing water is formed, and the limewater goes milky, showing that carbon dioxide is formed.

candle + oxygen → water + carbon dioxide

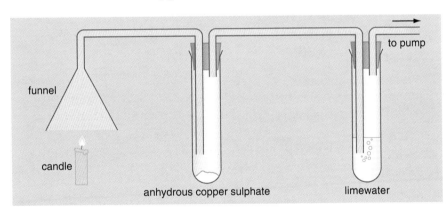

Figure 8 ◀

The level of the water in the bell jar rises when the candle burns because most of the carbon dioxide formed during burning dissolves in the water and the water formed condenses and only takes up a small volume.

The products from the burning of the candle are both **oxides** – an oxide is formed when oxygen combines with another element. The wax of the candle contains carbon and hydrogen and these elements combine with oxygen during combustion. Carbon combines with oxygen to form carbon dioxide. Hydrogen combines with oxygen to form hydrogen oxide – better known as water.

Test Yourself

13 In the experiment described above, the anhydrous copper sulphate might have turned blue because the air was damp or because pure water was formed when the candle burned. How could you modify the experiment to help you decide?

14 What two oxides are formed when a candle burns?

Fossil fuels

Coal, oil and gas are called **fossil fuels**, because they were formed from the bodies of dead animals and plants. Millions of years ago, plant and animal remains decayed and over time became to coal, oil and gas. Coal was mainly formed from land plants, while oil was mostly formed from plant and animal remains in the sea. These remains sank to the bottom of the ancient seas, which covered much of the Earth's surface, and were then buried by silt and mud. They formed layers that were rich in **organic material**. Organic material contains a lot of carbon.

Slowly, more and more layers were deposited, compressing the ones lower down and generating both heat and pressure. Out of contact with air and over long periods of time, complex reactions broke down the remains into simpler substances called **hydrocarbons**, which contain carbon and hydrogen only.

- Coal is a complicated solid hydrocarbon.
- Oil is a mixture of liquid hydrocarbons.
- **Natural gas** is mainly the gaseous hydrocarbon **methane**; natural gas occurs wherever oil is found.

The combustion of fossil fuels

Fuels are substances that release heat energy when they burn. A candle gives out heat energy when it burns, but not enough to make it really useful as a fuel. However, candles are very useful as sources of light. Most of the energy we use comes from the combustion of fossil fuels – we convert the heat energy they release on combustion to other forms of energy, mainly electricity.

Because all fossil fuels contain carbon and hydrogen, they all give carbon dioxide and water when they are burned:

$$\text{fossil fuel} + \text{oxygen} \xrightarrow{\text{combustion}} \text{water} + \text{carbon dioxide}$$

Methane is an important fossil fuel and it is the main constituent of natural gas. It burns in plenty of oxygen to give carbon dioxide and water:

$$\text{methane} + \text{oxygen} \rightarrow \text{carbon dioxide} + \text{water}$$

Other fuels

Although the most important fuels are fossil fuels, they do have one major drawback – they are **non-renewable**. Our need for energy is always increasing because there are more people who need energy and more vehicles than ever before. We are using up the reserves of fossil fuels much faster than they can be formed – remember they take millions of years to form.

The result will be that our reserves of fossil fuels will become exhausted and other fuels will have to be developed. In order to conserve stocks of fossil fuels, engine designers are improving the efficiency of car engines.

Ethanol as a fuel

Ethanol has the formula C_2H_5OH. Ethanol can be made from any sugar by a process called **fermentation**. In fermentation, yeast acts as a catalyst to convert sugar to ethanol and carbon dioxide.

$$\text{sugar} + \text{yeast} \xrightarrow{\text{catalyst}} \text{ethanol} + \text{carbon dioxide}$$

Ethanol burns to give carbon dioxide, water and a lot of heat. Ethanol can be used as a fuel in hot countries, such as Brazil, where sugar cane grows quickly. In Brazil, ethanol is added to the petrol to make it go further – this saves money on oil imports. The great advantage of ethanol is that it is a **renewable** fuel – it is always possible to grow more sugar cane to ferment.

Safety and fuels

All fuels burn easily – they are all flammable. Liquid fuels, such as ethanol and petrol, can be particularly hazardous. To use them safely in the laboratory the following rules must observed.

- Burn the fuels only in a burner of the correct design.
- Stand the burner on a heat-proof mat.
- Keep all naked flames away while pouring the fuel.
- Keep stoppers on the bottles when not actually pouring the fuel.
- Move bottles of fuel away when experimenting with lighted fuels.

The main risk is that a large amount of spilt fuel will catch fire – always have a fire extinguisher and fire blanket close at hand.

Test Yourself

15 What is meant by the term *fuel*?

16 How were fossil fuels formed?

17 Explain in your own words why fossil fuels are described as being 'non-renewable'.

18 Why is ethanol added to petrol in some countries?

Test Yourself

19 What safety precautions should be observed when doing laboratory experiments with fuels?

Summary

When you have finished studying this chapter, you should understand that:

- ✔ Chemical reactions take lots of different forms, from the explosion of a firework to the rotting of a piece of fruit.

- ✔ In chemical reactions reactants are converted to products.

- ✔ The products of a reaction look different from the reactants from which they were formed.

- ✔ Changes in appearance, the formation of gases and energy changes all provide evidence that a reaction has taken place.

- ✔ Burning requires oxygen.

- ✔ The products of burning are always oxides.

- ✔ Fuels are substances that give out heat when they burn.

- ✔ Fossil fuels are the most important fuels. They were formed from the remains of buried dead plants and animals millions of years ago.

- ✔ Fossil fuels give carbon dioxide and water when they burn.

- ✔ Fossil fuels are non-renewable and they will eventually run out.

End-of-Chapter Questions

1 Explain in your own words the following key terms you have met in this chapter:

reactants

products

corrosion

flammable

precipitate

oxide

organic material

hydrocarbon

natural gas

methane

non-renewable

renewable

2 Fred was given four mixtures to investigate – A, B, C and D.

A contains copper and sodium carbonate

B contains copper and zinc

C contains magnesium and zinc

D contains magnesium and sodium carbonate

Using hydrochloric acid as the only other reactant, devise a series of experiments to show that each mixture contains the stated substances.

3 A lighted candle was placed under a bell jar and the time taken for the candle to go out was recorded. The experiment was repeated using bell jars of different volumes. The results are shown in the table.

Volume of bell jar in cm³	Time taken for candle to go out in s
100	24
200	48
250	60
500	120

a) What general conclusion can you draw from these results?

b) i) Draw a graph of bell jar volume (horizontal axis) against time for candle to go out (vertical axis).

End-of-Chapter Questions continued

ii) Use your graph to estimate for how long a candle would burn in a gas jar of volume 400 cm³.

c) i) Explain what volume of gas you would expect to remain in the 500 cm³ bell jar after the candle had gone out.

ii) Explain what you would expect the gas remaining to be.

4 Andrea did some experiments to compare petrol and ethanol as fuels for heating water. Her apparatus is shown in the diagram.

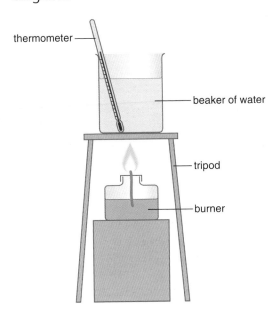

thermometer
beaker of water
tripod
burner

Here is Andrea's method for the experiment:

1 Put 25 cm³ of water in the beaker and record its temperature.

2 Weigh the spirit lamp containing petrol and place it under the beaker of water.

3 Light the spirit lamp and stir the water until its temperature has risen by 20 °C.

4 Re-weigh the spirit lamp.

5 Repeat steps 1 to 4 with ethanol in place of petrol in the spirit lamp.

Andrea's results are given in the table.

	Petrol	Ethanol
Mass of burner at start of experiment	25.31 g	24.22 g
Mass of burner at end of experiment	25.29 g	24.18 g
Mass of fuel burned		

a) Complete the table.

b) i) Use Andrea's results to explain which fuel was better.

ii) Petrol costs twice as much as ethanol per gram. Is it more economical to use petrol or ethanol as a fuel?

c) What advantage does ethanol have over petrol as a fuel in the long term?

d) Look at the design of Andrea's experiment and the procedure she used. Suggest any changes which could be made to improve the accuracy of the experiment.

e) Suggest what safety precautions should be observed during the experiment.

Reactions of acids and alkalis

Have you ever sucked on a piece of lemon or eaten a lemon sweet and then screwed up your face because it tasted so sour? The sour taste comes from the acid in the lemon. All acids taste sour. In fact the word 'acid' comes from the Latin word *acidus*, which means 'sour'. Acids are found in lots of places in nature – not just in lemons.

- Grapes contain tartaric acid, which gives wine its 'dry' taste.
- The 'sting' in stinging nettles comes from an acid. The nettles use the acids to protect themselves from being eaten by animals.
- Ants inject an acid called methanoic acid when they bite you. This is what irritates the skin and causes the stinging sensation.
- Some caterpillars contain an acid which makes them taste horrible. Birds soon learn not to eat them when they realise how bad they taste!

Acids

Organic acids

All of the acids that were mentioned above are **organic acids** because they are found in living things. They contain carbon and are usually weak acids. Many organic acids are found in food, drinks and medicines and are not hazardous.

- Aspirin is an acid; millions of aspirin tablets are taken daily throughout the world.
- Vinegar contains an organic acid called ethanoic acid.
- The acid in lemons, oranges, and other citrus fruits, is citric acid.
- Carbon dioxide gas dissolved in soft drinks makes them fizzy. The carbon dioxide forms a weak acid – carbonic acid.

Figure 1 ▲   All of these contain acids

Mineral acids

The acids usually found in the laboratory are **mineral acids**. They don't contain carbon atoms. Some examples of mineral acids are sulphuric acid (H_2SO_4), nitric acid (HNO_3) and hydrochloric acid (HCl). Although they can be harmful, mineral acids can also be very useful. You have hydrochloric acid in your stomach to help your digest your food.

The properties of acids

As well as tasting sour, acids also share other properties:

- they are **corrosive** (they burn the skin and dissolve metals)
- they can change the colour of **indicators** (see page 32)
- they can be **neutralised** by chemicals called alkalis (see page 34).

Extension box

The one thing that all acids have in common, and which can explain these common properties, is that they all release hydrogen ions in solution. These hydrogen ions can be written as H^+. By measuring how many hydrogen ions an acid releases in solution, we can tell whether the acid is **strong** or **weak**. Mineral acids are strong and release a lot of hydrogen ions. Organic acids are weak and only release a small number of hydrogen ions.

One thing to remember is that strong and weak acids are different from **concentrated** and **dilute** acids. You can make an acid more dilute by adding more water to it, but this won't change it from a strong acid to a weak acid.

Test Yourself

1   List four properties of acids.

2   What is the difference between an organic acid and a mineral acid?

3   Name two organic acids found in plants and one organic acid found in an animal.

4   Which acid is found in your stomach? What does it do?

5   Which ion do acids release in water? What do we call acids that release a lot of these ions?

Uses of acids

We make use of acids in lots of different ways:

- Sulphuric acid is used in drain cleaners and car batteries.
- Steel is treated with acid to remove surface rust before it is painted. Sulphuric acid is often used because it is cheap and is a very strong acid. If the rust was left on the steel and just painted over, the paint would flake off very easily and the rust would spread. Another acid that is used is phosphoric acid. This is often used to remove rust from car bodies.
- Baking powder is a mixture of baking soda and a solid acid, such as tartaric acid. No reaction happens between these two substances until they are added to water. When they are added to water, the tartaric acid reacts with the baking soda. This reaction produces carbon dioxide, which is a gas. We use baking powder when we make a cake because the carbon dioxide produced makes the cake rise.
- Limescale (calcium carbonate) can be removed from kettles, taps and baths with acids, all of which react with the calcium carbonate. For example, hydrochloric acid reacts with calcium carbonate as shown below:

$$\text{calcium carbonate} + \text{hydrochloric acid} \rightarrow \text{calcium chloride} + \text{carbon dioxide} + \text{water}$$

Word equations, like the one above, are a convenient way of summarising what has happened in a chemical reaction. You can find out how to write equations like these on page 16 of Chapter 2.

Alkalis

Alkalis are another group of chemicals. We can think of them as the chemical opposites of acids.

The first alkaline solutions were made by adding ash from wood fires to water and then filtering the mixture. In fact the word alkali came from the Arabic word for ash. Alkalis were recognised by the slippery, soapy feel they gave when rubbed on the skin. Alkalis feel soapy because they dissolve the natural grease and oil on your skin.

The commonest strong alkali in use in the laboratory is sodium hydroxide. Ammonia solution (sometimes called ammonium hydroxide) is a weak alkali.

Extension box

Just like acids, alkalis form particles when they dissolve in water. Acids release hydrogen ions but alkalis release hydroxide ions. We write these as OH^-. In the same way that you can have strong and weak acids, you can have strong or weak alkalis. We say an alkali is strong if it releases a lot of hydroxide ions in solution. Weak alkalis only release a small number of hydroxide ions.

Uses of alkalis

- Many household cleaners contain alkalis to dissolve grease from cookers and floors.
- Calcium hydroxide (also known as slaked lime) is added to soils to make them less acidic. It can also be added to lakes that have become too acidic as a result of acid rain. These are more examples of neutralisation reactions (see page 34).
- Sodium hydroxide is a very important alkali and is used in many manufacturing processes, such as the manufacture of paper, soap and ceramics.

Figure 2 ▲ All these products contain alkalis

Test Yourself

5   What ions are found in alkaline solutions?

6   Name two uses of alkalis.

31

The pH scale

The **pH scale** was invented in 1909 by the Swedish chemist Søren Sørenson. He worked for the Carlsberg company and he wanted to know about the acidity of beer the company was brewing.

The pH scale is used to show whether a solution is acidic or alkaline. It can also show how strong or weak the acids and alkalis are. The pH scale goes from 0 to 14.

- Acids have a pH of less than 7.
- Alkalis have a pH of more than 7.
- Neutral solutions, such as water, have a pH of 7.

pH

| 0 | 1 | 2 | 3 | 4 | 5 | 6 | 7 | 8 | 9 | 10 | 11 | 12 | 13 | 14 |

Neutral

strong acid   weak acid   weak alkali   strong alkali

Figure 3 ▲ The pH scale

Indicators

You can find out the pH of a solution in lots of different ways. For example, you might use a piece of equipment called a pH meter. This is an electrical instrument that can tell you the exact pH of a solution.

In your school laboratory, you are more likely to use **indicators**. These are solutions of dyes that are one colour in acids and a different colour in alkalis. Indicators can be used to tell whether a solution is acidic or alkaline. There are many indicators, but the common ones are shown in Table 1, together with their colours in acids and alkalis.

Figure 4 ► A pH meter

Indicator	Colour in acid	Colour in alkali
litmus	red	blue
phenolphthalein	colourless	pink
methyl orange	red	yellow

Table 1 ▲ Some common indicators

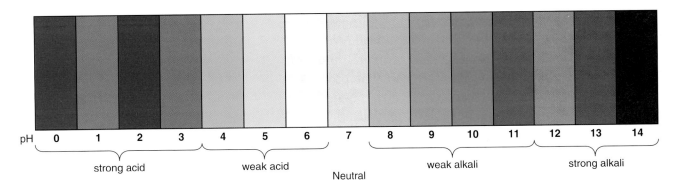

pH   0   1   2   3   4   5   6   7   8   9   10   11   12   13   14

strong acid   weak acid   weak alkali   strong alkali

Neutral

Figure 5 ▲   The pH scale and the different colours of universal indicator

Some vegetables contain indicators. Red cabbage is one example. The juice from red cabbage leaves is red in acids and turns blue in alkalis.

Universal indicator is a mixture of indicators which can be used to measure the acidity or alkalinity of a solution. The various indicators have been chosen so that universal indicator is a different colour at each point on the pH scale. Universal indicator is added to the solution to be tested, and the colour the indicator turns is compared with the colour on a chart to give the pH of the solution. Universal indicator can be used either as a paper strip or as a solution.

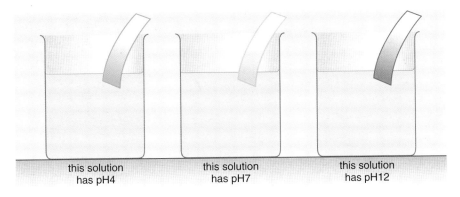

this solution has pH4   this solution has pH7   this solution has pH12

Figure 6 ▲   Universal indicator in use

Test Yourself

7   a)   Hydrochloric acid is a strong acid. What would you expect the pH in your stomach to be?
    b)   What colour would universal indicator turn in a solution of this pH?

8   What do you think the pH of the following would be:
    a)   ammonia solution
    b)   sodium hydroxide solution?

Neutralisation

Solutions of acids have a pH less than 7. Solutions of alkalis have a pH greater than 7. When an acid is mixed with an alkali, a neutral solution with a pH of 7 is produced. The process of mixing just enough alkali with an acid to give a neutral solution is called **neutralisation**. You can think of neutralisation as the acid cancelling the alkali out.

Neutralisation reactions can be very useful to us:

- Excess stomach acid can cause a lot of pain – this is often known as 'heartburn'. Heartburn can be relieved by taking tablets to neutralise the acid. These tablets often contain calcium carbonate or magnesium hydroxide.
- Soil has to be slightly alkaline if certain plants are to grow well. If the soil is too acidic, calcium hydroxide can be added to neutralise the acid and to make the soil alkaline.
- As we saw earlier, limescale removers are acidic. They remove the alkaline limescale from kettles and baths by reacting with it.

Figure 7 ▲ This farmer is adding lime to his fields to make the soil more alkaline

Extension box

Why do acids and alkalis neutralise each other?

We saw before that water is a neutral solution, with a pH of 7. As we know, acids contain hydrogen ions, H^+, and alkalis contain hydroxide ions, OH^-. When acids and alkalis are mixed, these two ions react together to form water:

$$\text{hydrogen ions} + \text{hydroxide ions} \rightarrow \text{water}$$

$$H^+(aq) + OH^-(aq) \rightarrow H_2O(l)$$

All neutralisations involve this reaction, whatever acid or alkali is used.

Reactions of acids

Acids react with many substances in neutralisation reactions. These reactions are very useful for making new substances, called **salts**.

Reactions of acids with alkalis

When an acid reacts with an alkali, the two products are a salt and water. The word equation for this reaction is:

acid + alkali → salt + water

The salt formed takes its name from the acid used to make it:

- *sulph*ates are made from *sulph*uric acid
- *nitr*ates are made from *nitr*ic acid
- *chlor*ides are made from hydro*chlor*ic acid.

For example:

hydrochloric acid + sodium hydroxide → sodium chloride + water

nitric acid + calcium hydroxide → calcium nitrate + water

Reactions of acids with reactive metals

When an acid reacts with a reactive metal, a salt is produced and hydrogen gas is given off. The general reaction is:

acid + reactive metal → salt + hydrogen

Zinc, iron and magnesium are reactive metals. They all react with acids to give hydrogen.

hydrochloric acid + zinc → zinc chloride + hydrogen

sulphuric acid + iron → iron sulphate + hydrogen

sulphuric acid + magnesium → magnesium sulphate + hydrogen

Copper is not as reactive as zinc, iron and magnesium and doesn't give hydrogen when treated with an acid. Silver is also less reactive than zinc, iron or magnesium and also does not react with acids.

Reactions of acids with metal oxides

When an acid reacts with a metal oxide, the products are always a salt and water. This reaction can be summarised as:

acid + metal oxide → salt + water

Some examples of this reaction are given below:

sulphuric acid + copper oxide → copper sulphate + water

nitric acid + zinc oxide → zinc nitrate + water

hydrochloric acid + magnesium oxide → magnesium chloride + water

Reactions of acids with carbonates

Acids react with carbonates to produce a salt, carbon dioxide and water. The general reaction is:

acid + carbonate → salt + water + carbon dioxide

For example:

hydrochloric + calcium → calcium + water + carbon
acid   carbonate chloride   dioxide

Notice that the full name of the salt depends on the acid used *and* the metal carbonate used, as shown in Table 2.

	Sulphuric acid	Hydrochloric acid	Nitric acid
Copper carbonate	copper sulphate	copper chloride	copper nitrate
Calcium carbonate	calcium sulphate	calcium chloride	calcium nitrate
Zinc carbonate	zinc sulphate	zinc chloride	zinc nitrate
Magnesium carbonate	magnesium sulphate	magnesium chloride	magnesium nitrate

Table 2 ▲ The salts produced when carbonates react with different acids

Test Yourself

9 Write down the word equation for the reactions between the following:
   a) magnesium oxide and sulphuric acid
   b) zinc carbonate and hydrochloric acid
   c) iron oxide and nitric acid
   d) zinc and hydrochloric acid

10 What do you think the name of the salt formed by a reaction between zinc oxide and ethanoic acid would be?

11 Complete the word equations for the following reactions:
   a) iron carbonate + hydrochloric acid →
   b) sodium carbonate + hydrochloric acid →
   c) potassium carbonate + nitric acid →

Working safely with acids

Many acids and alkalis can harm your skin and all of them are dangerous if they get into your eyes. You should be extremely careful when working with acids and alkalis in the laboratory.

Bottles containing chemicals may show one or more **hazard symbols** so that people know how to work with them safely, and how to deal properly with an accident.

When working with acids in the laboratory you must always:

- wear eye protection
- wear a laboratory coat or apron
- wear gloves if the acid is concentrated.

Dealing with spills and splashes

Acids become much less of a hazard when they are dilute. Spills and splashes should be dealt with by adding water or by mopping up the spill with a wet cloth. *You must wear gloves when doing this.*

Disposing of acids and alkalis safely

Excessive amounts of acids should not be allowed to reach the environment – living things can be harmed by them and soil can be made less fertile. If substances containing acids or alkalis have been used in the home, they should be flushed down the sink (if this is recommended) with plenty of water to dilute them.

a) harmful
e.g. 1M copper sulphate

b) irritant
e.g. 2M hydrochloric acid

c) corrosive
e.g. 1M sodium hydroxide

Figure 8 ▲ a) Harmful substances are just what they say on the label.
b) Irritant substances can cause redness and soreness on the skin.
c) Corrosive substances burn the skin and cause damage to it. Corrosive substances are particularly dangerous if they get into your eyes.

Summary

When you have finished studying this chapter, you should understand that:

- ✓ All acids have a sour taste.

- ✓ The pH scale allows the acidity/alkalinity of solutions to be compared.

- ✓ Neutral solutions have a pH of 7, acids have a pH less than 7 and alkalis have a pH greater than 7.

- ✓ Indicators are solutions of dyes that can be used to tell the pH of a solution.

- ✓ Acids and alkalis change the colour of indicators.

- ✓ Acids can be neutralised by alkalis. The products of this reaction are a salt and water.

- ✓ Acids react with reactive metals, forming a salt and hydrogen.

- ✓ Acids react with metal oxides, forming a salt and water.

- ✓ Acids react with carbonates, forming a salt, water and carbon dioxide.

- ✓ Acids and alkalis can be hazardous so care should be taken when working with them in the laboratory.

End-of-Chapter Questions

1 Explain in your own words the following key terms you have met in this chapter:

organic acid

mineral acid

strong acid

weak acid

alkali

pH scale

indicator

neutralise

corrosive

2 Sarah was doing some experiments on the pH of soil from different parts of the school grounds. She stirred up each soil sample with distilled water and then filtered the mixture before adding universal indicator solution. The colour of the indicator at various pH values is shown.

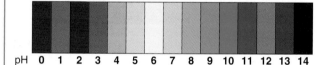

pH 0 1 2 3 4 5 6 7 8 9 10 11 12 13 14

Sarah's results

Soil sample from	Colour of universal indicator
near bicycle shed	yellow
on playing field	green
under trees near school	pale blue
by path near chemistry laboratory	red

a) Explain why Sarah had to filter the mixture before she added the indicator.

b) Complete the table below to show the pH of each soil sample.

Soil sample from	pH of soil sample
near bicycle shed	
on playing field	
under trees near school	
by path near chemistry laboratory	

c) Which sample was:

  i)   most acidic,

  ii) most alkaline,

  iii) neutral?

d) i)   Can you suggest an explanation for the pH of the soil from near the chemistry laboratory?

  ii) Name a substance which could be added to the soil near the chemistry laboratory to increase its pH. How would the substance do this?

e) James did a similar set of experiments but he used rain water not distilled water. All his pH values followed the same pattern as Sarah's, except they were all a bit lower. Can you suggest an explanation?

3 Marek wanted to make some copper sulphate from copper oxide. He wrote down some instructions, but he got them in the wrong order. He had also made a mistake in his instructions.

  A Allow the solution to cool.

  B Filter the solution.

  C Add copper oxide to hydrochloric acid until no more dissolves.

  D Dry the crystals.

  E Evaporate the solution to about half its volume.

End-of-Chapter Questions continued

a) Read his instructions and write them down in the correct order using the letters. The first one has been done for you.

C ___ ___ ___ ___

b) What was the other mistake in Marek's instructions?

c) Name the substance Marek would have made if he had followed his original instructions.

d) Write a word equation for the reaction to make copper sulphate.

e) Why was filtration used in the experiment?

f) What safety precautions should be taken while doing this experiment?

4 Andy decided to find out which indigestion tablet was the best value for money. The village chemist gave him five different tablets to try – V, W, X, Y and Z. The chemist worked out the cost of one tablet for Andy. All the tablets contained magnesium carbonate.

His plan was as follows:

A Take 25 cm³ of dilute hydrochloric acid and put it in a beaker.

B Add one of the tablets and measure the pH using universal indicator paper.

C Keep adding tablets and testing the pH until the solution has a pH of 7, when it will be neutral.

D Count how many tablets are needed to neutralise the acid.

E Repeat with the other four tablets.

Andy's results and the cost of each tablet are shown in the table.

Tablet	Number of tablets needed	Cost of each tablet
V	2	25p
W	5	12p
X	3	16p
Y	3	22p
Z	6	9p

a) Work out the total cost of neutralising the acid for each of the tablets.

b) Arrange the tablets in order of value for money, starting with the best and finishing with the worst.

c) What did Andy do to ensure that his test was a fair one?

d) The magnesium carbonate used in the tablets is in the form of a fine powder held together by a sugary mixture to make the tablets taste better. Why do you think that the magnesium carbonate was in the form of a fine powder?

4

Solutions

If you used a bucket to scoop up some sea water from a rock pool on a beach you might get a selection of different objects. There could be many things in your bucket: water, sand, seaweed, shellfish, pebbles, maybe even a fish! The contents of the bucket is what we call a **mixture**. A mixture is substances which are not chemically joined together, they can be separated into their different substances.

If we scoop out the larger objects, like the seaweed and pebbles, and put them back into the sea, our bucket will still contain a mixture of sand, sea water and small particles suspended in the water. Do you have any ideas how you could go about separating all the components of the mixture?

Filtering

The sand and the small suspended particles do not dissolve in water – they are insoluble. This means that the solid particles can be separated from the sea water by **filtration**. Filtration works because the very small holes in the filter paper (too small for you to see) let the sea water through, but hold back the larger solid particles (Figure 2).

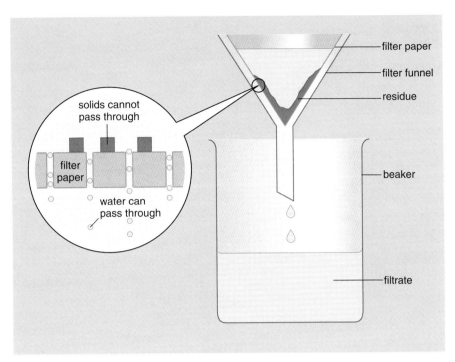

Figure 2 ▲ Filtration

So, you have scooped out the seaweed, shellfish, pebbles and fish and filtered off the sand, but you still need to separate the water from the substances dissolved in the water.

Solvents, solutes and solutions

Sea water tastes different from pure water because sea water has substances **dissolved** in it. The salty taste of sea water comes from the sodium chloride which is dissolved in the water– sodium chloride is soluble in water. The substance, which is dissolved in the water, in this case sodium chloride, is called the **solute** and the water is called the **solvent**. The solute and solvent together make up the **solution** – sea water.

When a substance dissolves, it is broken down into particles that are so small that they become invisible. The solute spreads out throughout the solvent. In sea water the particles of water and the particles of sodium chloride are distributed uniformly – there is the same amount of sodium chloride in every part of the solution.

Test Yourself

1 Write a short account of how to carry out filtration.

Figure 3 ▼ When salt dissolves in water, the particles of salt are broken down and spread out

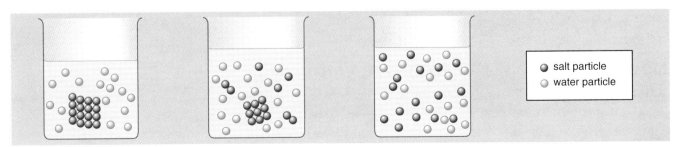

salt particle
water particle

- *Solute*: the substance that dissolves, e.g. sodium chloride
- *Solvent*: the liquid that the solute dissolves in, e.g. water
- *Solution*: the solute and the solvent together, e.g. sea water

The solute may seem to disappear when a solution is formed, but you can tell there is sodium chloride in sea water by the salty taste. You can also tell that the sodium chloride is still there by weighing the sodium chloride before it is added to the water and then weighing the solution after it has dissolved. When a solution is formed, mass is conserved – the mass of the solution equals the mass of the solvent *plus* the mass of the solute.

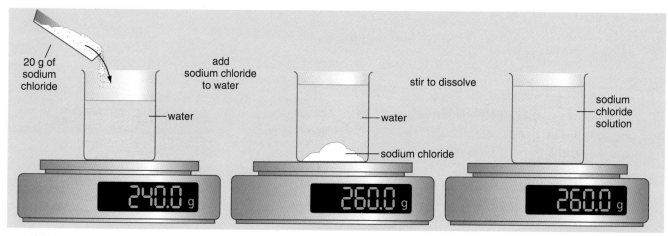

20 g of sodium chloride

add sodium chloride to water

stir to dissolve

water

water

sodium chloride

sodium chloride solution

240.0 g

260.0 g

260.0 g

Figure 4 ▲   Sodium chloride may seem to disappear, but it is still there.

Separating solutes and solvents

The sodium chloride in sea water can be obtained as a solid by evaporating off all the water – this is called evaporating to dryness. The water in the sea water is heated until it turns to steam, leaving behind the substances which were dissolved. The solid we are left with are crystals of sodium chloride. Crystals of sodium chloride form as the volume of the water is reduced. This is called **crystallisation**.

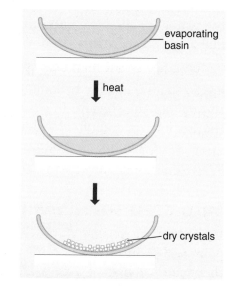

evaporating basin

heat

dry crystals

Figure 5 ▲   Evaporating a solution to dryness

Test Yourself

2   Explain how evaporation allows solid sodium chloride to be obtained from sea water.

How to get the water from sea water

When the sea water was evaporated, the sodium chloride was left, but the water was lost as water vapour into the air. To get the water from sea water you need to use the process called **distillation**.

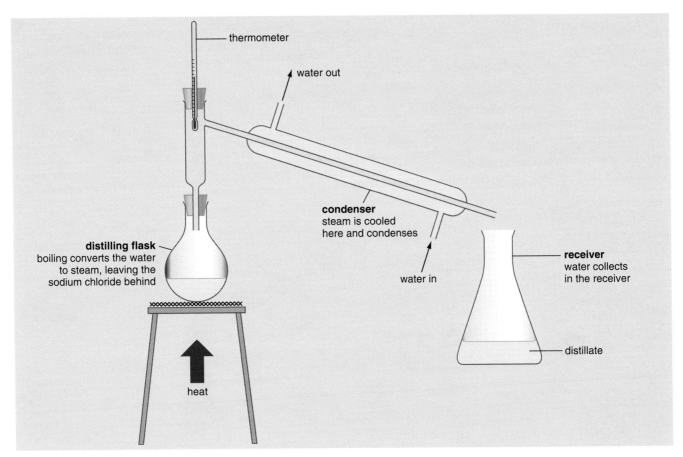

Figure 6 ▲ Distillation

Look at Figure 6. When the liquid in the flask is boiled the particles in the water are given more energy and can escape from the liquid. They **evaporate** to form steam (water vapour). The steam makes its way out of the flask and eventually reaches the condenser, where the steam is cooled. This cooling removes energy from the particles in the steam so they are able to attract each other enough to **condense** to form liquid water again. The sodium chloride stays behind in the flask because the temperature is not high enough to boil the sodium chloride.

Pure water can be made from any mixture that contains water, no matter how impure the mixture is. Many people who have been stranded without water in deserts owe their survival to this method. They were able to get pure water from muddy ponds, or even from the cooling system of their car.

Saturated solutions

If you keep on adding sodium chloride to a beaker of water, a point will come when no more sodium chloride will dissolve. Once this point has been reached, any more sodium chloride added remains as a solid and does not dissolve. Solutions in which no more solute will dissolve are known as **saturated solutions**.

Test Yourself

3   Explain, in your own words, how a condenser works.

4   Explain how distillation can separate mixtures of liquids.

Extension box

How is solubility affected by temperature?

The **solubility** of a solute is the number of grams of the solute that dissolve in 100 g of water at a certain temperature. Figure 7 shows how much copper sulphate will dissolve in 100 g of water at a range of temperatures. Notice that the amount of copper sulphate that can dissolve increases as the temperature of the water increases.

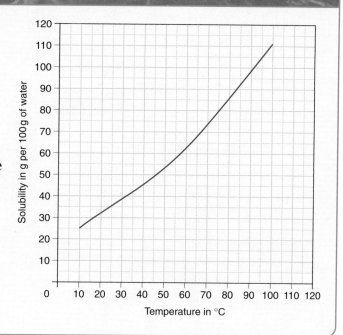

Figure 7 ▶ The solubility curve for copper sulphate

A solubility curve allows you to obtain a range of information.

1 Determination of the solubility at any temperature. Look at Figure 7: move upwards from the chosen temperature on the temperature axis until you meet the solubility curve and then read off the corresponding solubility from the other axis. For example, the solubility of copper sulphate at 45 °C is 50 g per 100 g of water.

2 Determination of the temperature at which crystals will form. If a solution is cooled, a temperature will be reached at which crystals are first seen. This is the temperature at which crystallisation begins. Exactly what this temperature is depends on the amount of solute dissolved. Suppose that there are 30 g of copper sulphate in solution with 100 g of water: moving parallel to the temperature axis on Figure 7, we meet the curve at about 17 °C. At this temperature (and below) crystals of copper sulphate will be present.

3 Determination of the mass of crystals formed on cooling a particular solution. If you know how much copper sulphate will dissolve at two different temperatures, it is easy to work out what mass of copper sulphate crystals will form on cooling from one temperature to another. Again using Figure 7, you can see that a saturated solution of copper sulphate in 100 g of water at 80 °C will contain 85 g of copper sulphate. Now cool this solution to 40 °C. The solubility at this new temperature is 45 g per 100 g of water. Therefore 40 g of copper sulphate will crystallise out of solution.

5 What is the solubility of copper sulphate at:
  a) 30 °C
  b) 90 °C?

6 What is the lowest temperature at which:
  a) 100 g of water will dissolve 60 g of copper sulphate?
  b) 50 g of water will dissolve 40 g of copper sulphate?

7 At what temperature will crystals form when a solution containing 85 g of copper sulphate in 100 g of water is cooled from 100 °C?

8 What mass of copper sulphate crystals form when a solution containing 25 g of copper sulphate in 25 g of water is cooled from 90 °C to 50 °C?

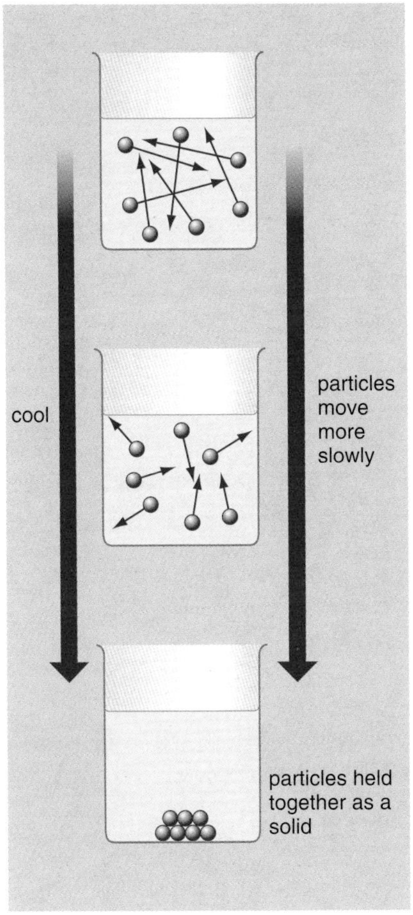

Why do crystals form when solutions are cooled?

Particle theory (see Chapter 1) helps to explain why crystals form when solutions are cooled. Crystals form when a solution is cooled because the solute particles have less energy. The forces between the particles are then strong enough to keep them in a fixed arrangement, forming crystals. Heating up the mixture reverses the change and the solute crystals dissolve again.

cool

particles move more slowly

particles held together as a solid

Figure 8 ▲ Cooling a solution allows crystals to form

Salt

Uses of salt

Salt (sodium chloride) has a great many uses. Salt has always been very valuable, it has even been used as a currency in some areas of the world. The Austrian city of Salzburg grew rich in mediaeval times from the sale of salt. The salt trade in Britain began in Roman times when people extracted salt from natural springs. The term 'wyche' at the end of a place name means that there is a salt spring there. So Northwich, Middlewich and Nantwich are all named after salt springs.

- Sodium chloride is an essential part of your diet as it is involved in many processes in your body, including sweating.
- The food industry uses a lot of sodium chloride as a flavour enhancer and preservative.
- The chemical industry has many uses for sodium chloride and the substances manufactured from it. Some of these uses are summarised in Figure 9.

9 Name three things made using:
  a) sodium hydroxide
  b) chlorine.

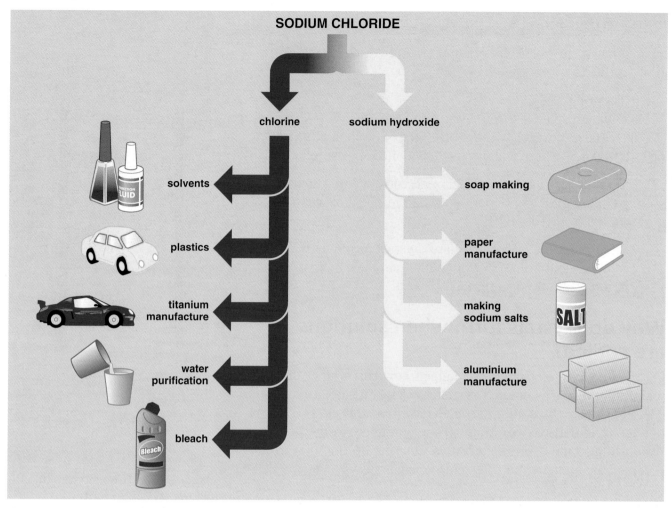

Figure 9 ▲ Some industrial uses for sodium chloride

Sources of salt

Rock salt is found underground in places where water cannot reach. It is dug out of the ground using mechanical diggers and brought to the surface. Rock salt is a mixture of sodium chloride, sand and gravel.

Rock salt is put on the roads in cold weather to melt the ice so that vehicles can use the roads safely. The gravel in the rock salt helps car tyres to grip the road better.

Test Yourself

10 Why is rock salt only found underground in places water cannot reach?

11 Describe how you could get solid sodium chloride from a sample of rock salt.

Figure 10 ▲ Winsford Rock Salt Mine in Cheshire. The tunnels in the mine are 100 miles long, and the mine can produce 1.5 million tonnes of rock salt a year.

Figure 11 ▲ Salt being added to snowy roads by a gritter

Sodium chloride can also be obtained by solution mining. Solution mining involves pumping water into underground salt deposits. The sodium chloride dissolves and the solution is pumped up to the surface and then evaporated to get the solid sodium chloride.

In some parts of the world there are huge underground deposits of sodium chloride in salt mines. Mining of rock salt in Britain began in the 17th century. Winsford Rock Salt Mine in Cheshire opened in 1844. It produces salt that is used to grit icy roads.

Sea salt is obtained from sea water by evaporation. It is mainly used in cooking.

Figure 12 ▲ Salt is obtained from sea water by evaporation in large salt pans

Ideas and Evidence

Separating coloured substances

In 1906 a Russian botanist named Mikhail Tswett published details of some experiments he had carried out on the coloured material in the leaves of green plants.

Tswett had crushed the leaves and mixed them with a solvent called petroleum ether to dissolve the coloured material. He then poured this solution into a glass column packed with powdered chalk. The solution formed a thin layer at the top of the column. Tswett then poured more petroleum ether onto the top of the column and opened the tap at the bottom of the column to let the solvent run through.

As the solvent moved down the column, bands of different colours formed at different distances down the column. Each of the coloured bands was due to a different substance in the coloured material from the leaf. Because the separated substances on his column were detected by observing their colours, Tswett named his new technique **chromatography**, from two Greek words meaning 'colour' and 'writing'. The Russian word 'tswett' actually means colour, maybe he named it after himself.

Chromatography

Chromatography and the particle model

In Tswett's experiments, the different coloured plant pigments could either stick to the chalk in the column, or be carried down by the solvent flowing down the column. Chromatography works because different substances dissolve to different extents in the moving solvent. Those substances that are very soluble in the solvent will be carried faster than those substances that dissolve less well. Using chromatography, the different coloured plant pigments could be separated.

Test Yourself

12 Explain, using the particle model, how chromatography can separate mixtures of substances.

Paper chromatography

Chromatography can be carried out using paper instead of glass tubes packed with chalk. The normal set up for a **paper chromatography** experiment at school is shown in Figure 14.

Individual spots of the coloured substances to be used are placed on a line drawn close to the bottom of the paper. The paper is then hung in a beaker so that it just dips into the solvent in the beaker. The solvent is absorbed by the paper and drawn upwards, taking each coloured spot with it.

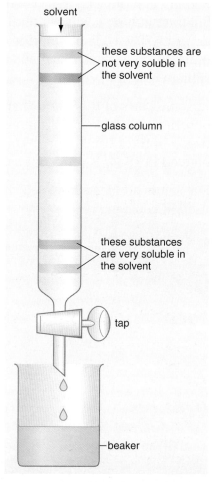

Figure 13 ▲ Chromatography

The solvent is drawn up by capillary action – the solvent is sucked into tiny spaces between the fibres of the paper. Kitchen towel soaks up spilt liquids in the same way.

If there is more than one substance in the coloured spot, each substance will be drawn up the paper at different speeds and so several blobs of colour will appear at different points on the paper. Just before the solvent reaches the top of the paper the paper is removed from the beaker and allowed to dry. The finished result is a **chromatogram**.

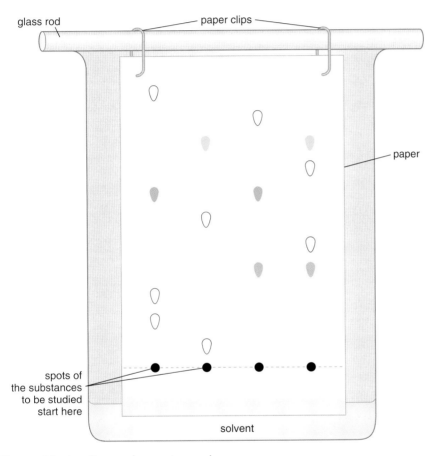

Figure 14 ▲   Paper chromatography

Identifying components of mixtures

In Figure 15 four substances A, B, C and D were started at the bottom of the paper. By looking at the completed chromatogram, some conclusions can be drawn.

- Substances A and C are the same because they separate into four spots, all of which are the same.
- Substance B is also a mixture of four substances, one of which is different from those in A and C.
- Substance D is a mixture of only three substances, and has a yellow substance in it which is not found in substance A, B or C.

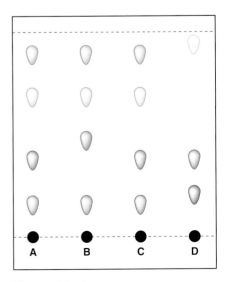

Figure 15 ▲

Separating colourless substances

Given the fact that chromatography means 'colour writing', it might seem odd to try to separating colourless substances using the technique. However, there are various methods that can be used to make colourless substances visible.

Amino acids

Amino acids are important biological molecules, but they are all colourless. They can be separated by paper chromatography, but it is impossible to see the spots on the paper. To make the spots visible, the chromatogram is sprayed with a solution of a substance called ninhydrin. This makes the spots visible as the individual amino acids turn purple in contact with ninhydrin. Ninhydrin is called a locating agent.

This technique was used by Frederick Sanger to help him work out the amino acid sequence in the protein insulin – he was awarded the 1958 Nobel Prize for Chemistry for this work.

The ingredients in painkillers

Many painkillers, or analgesics to give them their technical name, contain colourless substances. Examples are aspirin and ibuprofen. These substances appear colourless in visible light but look coloured under ultraviolet light. They fluoresce, giving out visible light, so the position of the spots on the paper can be marked in pencil. The chromatogram can then be studied later in normal light.

Uses of chromatography

We have already seen one use of chromatography – showing that two substances (A and C in Figure 15) are the same. However, we can do more than this.

If we have some idea of what a mixture might have in it, we can compare the chromatogram of the mixture with the chromatograms of the individual substances.

Many foods are coloured artificially to make them look more appealing to consumers. For example, orange squash is often coloured using dyes such as tartrazine, Sunset Yellow or Orange GGN. To find out which dyes have been used in a sample of orange squash we must compare the chromatogram of the orange squash with chromatograms of the three pure dyes. In Figure 16, the spots from the orange squash tested match those from tartrazine and Sunset Yellow. We can conclude that these dyes were used to colour this type of orange squash.

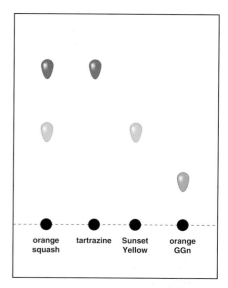

Figure 16 ▲

Summary

When you have finished studying this chapter, you should understand that:

✔ A solution results when a solute dissolves in a solvent.

✔ Filtration separates solids from liquids.

✔ Evaporation can be used to remove the solvent from a solution.

✔ Distillation separates liquids from solutions.

✔ Solutes become more soluble as the temperature increases.

✔ Chromatography separates the components of a mixture.

End-of-Chapter Questions

1 Explain in your own words the following key terms you have met in this chapter:

mixture   evaporate
filtration   condense
dissolved   saturated solution
solute   crystallisation
solvent   solubility
solution   chromatography
distillation   chromatogram

2 Copy and complete the table below.

Method	Used to separate	Example
	insoluble solids from liquids or solutions	
crystallisation		salt crystals from sea water
distillation	the solvent from a solution	
paper chromatography		

3 Describe how you would obtain:

a) salt crystals from sandy sea water

b) water from sandy sea water.

4 The following table shows the solubility of sugar in water.

Temperature in °C	Solubility in g per 100 g of water
20	204
30	219
40	238
50	260
60	287
70	320
80	362
90	416

a) What general trend in solubility do these figures show?

b) About how many times more soluble is sugar at 90 °C compared to 20 °C?

c) What weight of solid sugar will be formed when a saturated solution containing sugar and 100 g of water is cooled from 80 °C to 70 °C?

End-of-Chapter Questions continued

d) Plot a graph of temperature (x-axis) against solubility (y-axis), drawing the best curve through the points.

e) What is the solubility of sugar at 75 °C?

f) Use your graph to estimate the solubility of sugar at 100 °C.

5 A teacher gave the class the following instructions to extract the green colour from oak, yew and willow leaves.

Step 1 Chop a handful of leaves from each tree into small pieces.

Step 2 Add ethanol to the chopped leaves and stir well for 2 minutes.

Step 3 Filter off the leaves.

Step 4 Carry out paper chromatography on each of the coloured extracts, using ethanol as the solvent.

a) How did pupils get as much of the green colour out of the leaves as possible?

b) What else could have been done to help the extraction process? Explain how these extra steps would help.

c) Describe how you would carry out the paper chromatography experiment to find out if the green colour in all three leaves was due to the same substance.

6 Sue was given a lump of rock salt by her teacher. She was then asked to write a plan for experiments too get as much pure solid sodium chloride as possible from the lump of rock salt.

Here is Sue's plan.

Step A Take a beaker of cold water and add the lump of rock salt. Stir the lump around in the water.

Step B Filter off the lump of rock salt.

Step C Evaporate all the water to get sodium chloride crystals.

Step D Dry the crystals.

a) Suggest improvements to Step A in Sue's plan. Explain why your changes would allow more sodium chloride to be obtained from the lump of rock salt.

b) Explain why the crystals obtained in Step C would not be very pure. How could Step C be changed to improve the purity of the crystals?

c) Sue's lump of rock salt weighed 3.5 g and she got 2.0 g of sodium chloride crystals from it.

i) What mass of insoluble substances were in the lump of rock salt?

ii) What percentage of the rock salt was sodium chloride?

5

Atoms, elements and compounds

Look around your classroom and make a list of some of the different materials you can see. Your list might be something like this:

- aluminium
- brick
- glass
- iron
- paper
- plastic
- wood.

These materials can be arranged in many different ways. You could group together all the metals, or all the materials that you can easily bend or all the materials you can see through, and so on.

There is another way of arranging materials that depends on their chemical properties, on whether they are **elements** or **compounds**. Elements are substances that cannot be split into anything simpler.

Compounds are substances made from different elements joined together.

Figure 1 ▲ All the substances in the classroom are elements or compounds

Test Yourself

1 Make a list of as many properties of each of the substances in the list above as you can. You may like to use the following questions as a starting point:
 a) Is the substance hard?
 b) Does the substance bend easily?
 c) Is the substance magnetic?
 d) Can you see through the substance?
 e) What would happen if you put the substance in a Bunsen flame?
 f) Which of the substances float on water?
 g) What would happen if you hit the substance with a hammer?

	He helium
H hydrogen	

Li lithium	Be beryllium											B boron	C carbon	N nitrogen	O oxygen	F flourine	Ne neon
Na sodium	Mg magnesium											Al aluminium	Si silicon	P phosphorus	S sulphur	Cl chlorine	Ar argon
K potassium	Ca calcium	Sc scandium	Ti titanium	V vanadium	Cr chromium	Mn manganese	Fe iron	Co cobalt	Ni nickel	Cu copper	Zn zinc	Ga gallium	Ge germanium	As arsenic	Se selenium	Br bromine	Kr krypton
Rb rubidium	Sr strontium	Y yttrium	Zr zirconium	Nb niobium	Mo molybdenum	Tc technetium	Ru ruthenium	Rh rhodium	Pd palladium	Ag silver	Cd cadmium	In indium	Sn tin	Sb antimony	Te tellurium	I iodine	Xe xenon
Cs caesium	Ba barium	La lanthanum	Hf hafnium	Ta tantalum	W tungsten	Re rhenium	Os osmium	Ir iridium	Pt platinum	Au gold	Hg mercury	Tl thallium	Pb lead	Bi bismuth	Po polonium	At astatine	Rn radon
Fr francium	Ra radium	Ac actinium															

| Ce
cerium | Pr
praseodymium | Nd
neodymium | Pm
promethium | Sm
samarium | Eu
europium | Gd
gadolinium | Tb
terbium | Dy
dysprosium | Ho
holmium | Er
erbium | Tm
thulium | Yb
ytterbium | Lu
lutetium |
| Th
thorium | Pa
protactinium | U
uranium | | | | | | | | | | | |

Figure 2 ▲ The Periodic Table

Elements

The surprising thing is that although all the materials in your classroom have very different properties, they are all made from one or more **elements**. There are 92 naturally occurring elements: their symbols and names are shown in Figure 2. This table is called the Periodic Table, and we will meet it again later (page 58). The Periodic Table is a useful list of all the elements. (Another 23 elements can be made artificially – the best known artificial element is plutonium.)

An element is made up of **atoms**. An atom is the smallest amount of an element that can exist. The word *atom* comes from Greek and means 'can't be cut'.

Elements differ a great deal in their properties – they look different and they can be solids, liquids or gases.

Figure 3 ▲ At room temperature: a) chlorine is a gas, b) bromine is a liquid, c) carbon is a solid, d) mercury is a liquid, e) aluminium is a solid and f) sulphur is a solid

The list at the beginning of this chapter contains two elements – iron and aluminium. Iron contains only atoms of iron and aluminium contains only atoms of aluminium.

Metals and non-metals

One very important way of arranging elements is into two groups – **metals** and **non-metals**. Iron and aluminium are both metals. Chlorine, bromine and carbon are examples of non-metals.

Metals have a number of properties that enable you to decide if an element is a metal or not. Metals:

- are solids with high melting and boiling points (except mercury which is a liquid to room temperature)
- are strong
- conduct electricity
- can be hammered into different shapes (are malleable) and can be pulled into wires (are ductile)
- have high densities.

As a result of their properties, metals have a number of different uses.

Figure 5 ▲ Metals, such as copper, conduct electricity and can be shaped into long wires

Figure 4 ▲ Metals can hold large weights without breaking; iron is often used to build bridges

Non-metals, on the other hand, tend to have very varied properties:

- some are solids, some are liquids, some are gases
- they do not conduct electricity
- many break easily when hit.

There are a few exceptions to these properties, such as the liquid metal mercury and the non-metal graphite that conducts electricity.

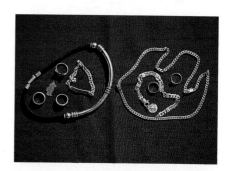

Figure 6 ▲ Metals, such as gold, silver and platinum, are shiny and do not wear away, so they are often used to make jewellery

As a result of their properties, non-metals are used for many different things.

Figure 7 ◄ This tennis racket is made from graphite, a form of carbon

Symbols

To save having to write the full name of every element and compound, scientists have given every element its own symbol. It is these symbols that are used in the Periodic Table. Table 1 contains the names and symbols of some of the common elements.

Element	Symbol	Element	Symbol
aluminium	Al	mercury	Hg
argon	Ar	nitrogen	N
calcium	Ca	oxygen	O
carbon	C	phosphorus	P
chlorine	Cl	potassium	K
copper	Cu	silicon	Si
fluorine	F	silver	Ag
hydrogen	H	sodium	Na
iron	Fe	sulphur	S
magnesium	Mg	zinc	Zn

Table 1 ▲ Some elements and their symbols

Some of the symbols are the first letter of the element's name, for example:

- carbon, C
- fluorine, F
- hydrogen, H
- nitrogen, N
- oxygen, O
- phosphorus, P
- sulphur, S.

Sometimes two letters from the element's name have to be used to tell it apart from other elements that start with the same letter, for example:

- aluminium, Al
- argon, Ar
- calcium, Ca
- chlorine, Cl
- silicon, Si.

Some symbols do not relate to the element's modern name. These symbols may come from other languages, such as Greek or Latin. Here are some examples:

- copper = Cu, from the Latin *cuprum*, the name for the island of Cyprus where copper was mined
- mercury = Hg, from the Latin *hydrargyrum*, meaning liquid silver
- potassium = K, from the Latin *kalium* (potassium carbonate)
- silver = Ag, from the Latin for silver *argentum*
- sodium = Na, from the Latin *natrium* (sodium carbonate).

The symbols can be combined to show the elements that are present in a compound. For example, sodium chloride is a compound that contains one atom of sodium and one atom of chlorine. Its symbol is NaCl. Carbon dioxide contains one atom of carbon and two atoms of oxygen. Its symbol is CO_2.

Ideas and Evidence — The search for patterns in the elements

During the nineteenth century, as more and more elements were discovered, scientists attempted to find similarities in their properties and reactions.

The Russian chemist Dmitri Mendeleev (1834–1907) made the most successful attempts. In 1869 he arranged the elements that were then known in order of increasing atomic weight to give the first Periodic Table.

Ideas and Evidence continued

The elements fell into families (named 'groups') with similar properties. He used the fact that elements combine to give compounds with a fixed composition to put them in the right group.

For example, Mendeleev found the compounds formed when elements react with oxygen to be very useful in placing the elements in groups. He correctly put carbon (C) and silicon (Si) in the same group because they both formed dioxides with a similar formula, CO_2 and SiO_2, even though the oxides had very different properties.

Mendeleev's early Periodic Tables were inaccurate because not all the naturally occurring elements had been discovered at that time. Further work led to the modern form of the Periodic Table, which is so useful to chemists today. Mendeleev realised that there were 'gaps' in his Periodic Table. He correctly predicted that scandium (Sc) and gallium (Ga) would be discovered to fill in some of these gaps. He even predicted the properties of these elements before they were discovered.

The Periodic Table of elements

All the elements, both metals and non-metals, are shown in the Periodic Table. The elements in the Periodic Table can be represented by a symbol. You may notice that similar elements are grouped together. For example, all the metals are found on one side of the table and all the non-metals one the other.

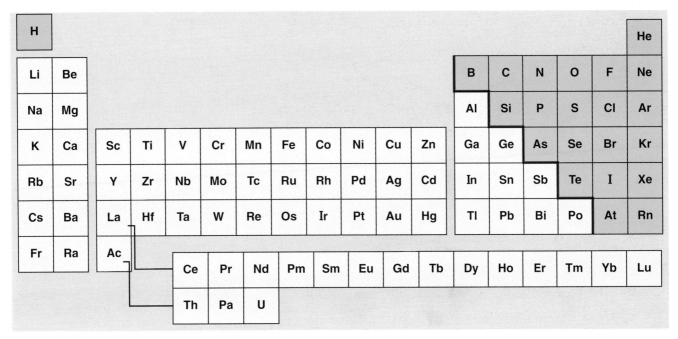

Figure 8 ▲ The position of the metals (yellow) and non-metals (green) in the Periodic Table

Groups and periods

The form of the Periodic Table suggested by Mendeleev arranged the elements into vertical columns called **groups**. Elements in the same group have very similar properties. For example, the elements in Group 1 are all very reactive silvery metals with low melting points.

The elements in the same group form compounds with similar formulae. For example, carbon and silicon in Group 4 both react with oxygen to give compounds containing two oxygen atoms for every carbon or silicon atom.

$$\text{carbon } + \text{ oxygen } \rightarrow \text{carbon dioxide } (CO_2)$$

$$\text{silicon } + \text{ oxygen } \rightarrow \text{silicon dioxide } (SiO_2)$$

The Periodic Table also contains horizontal rows, running from left to right, called **periods**.

Test Yourself

2 Are metals on the left or right of the Periodic Table?

3 Write down the symbol for each of these elements:
a) aluminium
b) carbon
c) helium
d) iron
e) magnesium
f) oxygen
g) sodium
h) sulphur.

4 Write down the physical state (solid, liquid or gas) of each of these elements at room temperature:
a) bromine
b) fluorine
c) iodine
d) lead
e) mercury
f) nitrogen
g) potassium.

Look at the website http://www.chemicalelements.com/

5 Use this site to find out the properties of the elements in Group 4. Find out:
a) the melting point
b) the boiling point
c) state at room temperature.

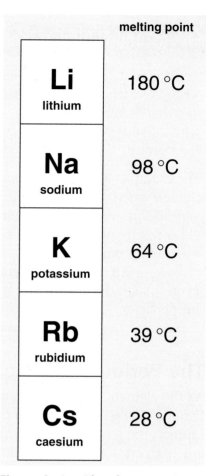

	melting point
Li lithium	180 °C
Na sodium	98 °C
K potassium	64 °C
Rb rubidium	39 °C
Cs caesium	28 °C

Figure 9 ▲ The elements of Group 1

6 Write down the name and symbol for an element that is:
  a) a liquid metal at room temperature
  b) a red liquid at room temperature
  c) very unreactive
  d) found in coal
  e) used to make soft drink cans
  f) used for wiring in the home
  g) used to make jewellery
  h) a poisonous gas
  i) burns in air to form water
  j) the most abundant gas in air
  k) magnetic
  l) a yellow solid
  m) found underneath potassium in the Periodic Table
  n) found to the right of carbon in the Periodic Table.

Ideas and Evidence   The structure of the atom

You have read that atoms are the smallest amount of an element that can exist. However atoms are made of even smaller 'sub-atomic' particles called protons, neutrons and electrons.

In 1897 a scientist called J J Thomson discovered the electron, which he found had a negative charge. He knew that atoms were neutral, so he realised that there must be something else inside the atom with a positive charge. In 1904 he suggested the first model of the atom. This model was called the 'plum pudding model' because it showed a sphere of positive charge with the negatively charged electrons randomly arranged inside it like the fruit in a plum pudding.

However a student of Thomson's, called Ernest Rutherford, decided that this model was not correct. In 1912 he proposed that the positively charged part was in the centre of the atom, which he called the nucleus. Rutherford's model of the atom showed a positively charged nucleus with the electrons at rest surrounding it.

A few years later Neils Bohr realised that the electrons had to be moving to stop them being attracted to the nucleus and came up with the

model of the atom that we still use today. This showed the nucleus at the centre of the atom with the electrons moving in rings around it, a bit like planets orbiting the sun.

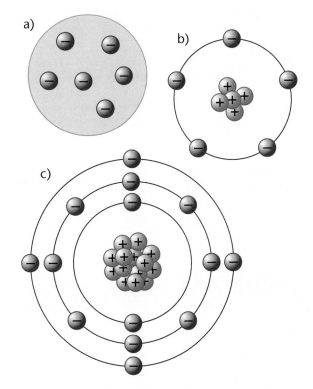

Figure 10 ▲   a) J J Thomson's atom model,
b) Ernest Rutherford's atom model, and
c) Neils Bohr's atom model

Extension box

The order of the elements in the Periodic Table

We have read that atoms are the smallest amount of an element that can exist. However, atoms *are* made of smaller 'sub-atomic' particles: protons, neutron and electrons.

The Periodic Table is not a random list of the chemical elements. The order of the elements depends on the number of protons in their atoms. The Periodic Table is a list of the elements in order of increasing number of protons. Arranged in this way they fall naturally into vertical groups of elements that have very similar chemical properties.

Compounds

We saw earlier that the list of substances you could find in your classroom (aluminium, brick, glass, iron, paper, plastic, wood) contains two elements – iron and aluminium. All the other substances in the list are **compounds** or mixtures of compounds. Compounds are formed when two or more elements combine together. The atoms of the elements are held together by forces of attraction called chemical bonds. Compounds and mixtures are discussed in more detail in Chapter 6.

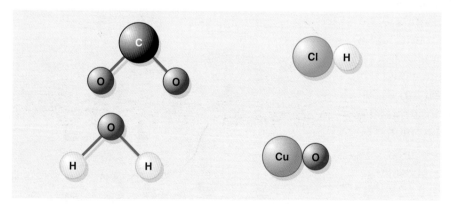

Figure 11 ▲ Carbon dioxide, water, hydrogen chloride and copper oxide are compounds

Test Yourself

7 What is the difference between an element and a compound?

8 What is the difference between an element and an atom?

The same atoms can join together in many different ways to make very different compounds. For example, methane contains only carbon atoms and hydrogen atoms. Methane is found in natural gas and is a gas at room temperature. Polythene, which also contains only carbon atoms and hydrogen atoms (but joined together in a very different way) is a solid at room temperature and is the compound from which plastic bags are made.

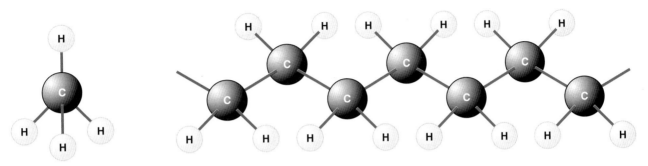

a methane molecule

a small section of a polythene molecule

Figure 12 ▲

The assembly of atoms in a compound is called a **molecule**. Molecules can be very simple or incredibly complicated – here are some examples:

- nitrogen: this gas makes up 78% of the air on Earth
- ethanoic acid: this liquid is found in vinegar
- octane: this liquid is found in petrol
- DDT: this solid was used as an insecticide
- cholesterol: this solid causes problems in your arteries.

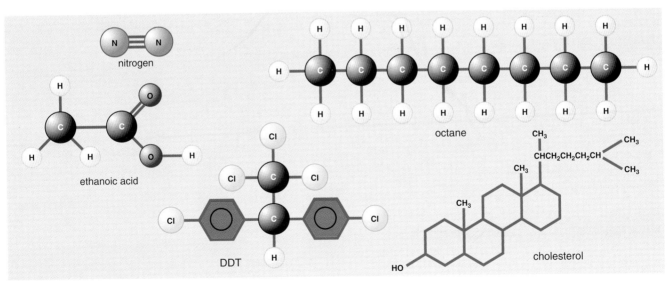

Figure 13 ▲ The structures of some molecules

We can summarise the formation of molecules from atoms as follows:

$$\text{atoms of elements} \xrightarrow{\text{chemical reaction}} \text{molecules of new compounds}$$

9   What is a molecule?

Elements around you

If you look around your school you may find the following solid elements in use:

- aluminium – handrails on stairs, window frames and mirrors
- copper – for electrical wiring and water pipes
- gold and silver – in jewellery and the plating on pen tops and watches
- iron – in metal table and chair legs and window frames
- silicon – out of sight in the microchips in calculators and computers.

You will be breathing some elements that are gases in the air:

- argon
- nitrogen
- oxygen.

You need to note that the atoms in some non-metallic elements join together to form molecules. Examples are nitrogen, N_2, and oxygen, O_2. Notice that each molecule contains more than one atom, but the atoms they contain are the same. Other elements that form molecules are sulphur, S_8, and chlorine, Cl_2.

Summary

When you have finished studying this chapter, you should understand that:

✔ The smallest particle of an element is an atom of that element.

✔ All the atoms in a sample of an element are the same.

✔ Elements can be classified as either metals or non-metals.

✔ All the known elements and their symbols are shown in the Periodic Table.

✔ Compounds are made of two or more different atoms joined together by chemical bonds.

✔ Molecules are two or more atoms joined together by chemical bonds.

✔ Some elements exist as molecules.

✔ Atoms are made up of sub-atomic particles called protons, neutrons and electrons.

✔ In atoms, electrons orbit the nucleus, which has a positive charge.

End-of-Chapter Questions

1 Explain in your own words the following key terms you have met in this chapter:

element

atom

metal

non-metal

group

period

compound

molecule

2 Here are the melting points of some elements.

Element	Melting point in °C
A	1890
B	327
C	−7
D	113
E	650
F	−249
G	64
H	1535
I	−157
J	660

a) Which letters might represent metals?

b) Which letters might represent non-metals?

c) i) Which elements from your list of metals are 'doubtful'?

ii) Explain your choice.

iii) How could you show that these 'doubtful' elements really were metals?

6 Compounds and mixtures

Many things we meet in everyday life are mixtures. Some mixtures, like the cooked breakfast shown in the picture, are easy to separate. We can see the large particles – the fried egg, the sausage and the bacon – that make up the mixture and they can simply be separated by hand. When the particles in a mixture of solids are smaller, separation becomes more difficult. Soil is a mixture: it is easy to pick out the bigger stones, but almost impossible to separate the smaller particles.

The important thing about mixtures is that the components of a mixture are not chemically joined together. If the components were separated, they would have the same properties and behave exactly as they did before mixing took place. For example, a mixture of sulphur powder and iron filings can be separated using a magnet.

Figure 1 ▲ Separating sulphur powder and iron filings

Air as a mixture

Exactly what a mixture contains can vary a lot; we say that a mixture does not have a fixed composition. Consider air as an example of a mixture: air is mostly a mixture of nitrogen (78%) and oxygen (21%) but it contains other things too.

- In a busy city the air might contain lot of carbon monoxide from cars.
- In a rural area the air could contain more seeds and pollen.
- Over the sea the air may contain a lot of water vapour.
- There also may be bigger, much more visible things in this mixture, such as aircraft, birds, bees and flies.

Test Yourself

1   Name three mixtures found in the home. What is each used for?

Ideas and Evidence

Air as a mixture – the work of Sir William Ramsay

During the 1890s, Sir William Ramsay (1852–1916) carried out a series of experiments that resulted in the discovery of several new elements.

Ramsay passed an electric spark through some air contained in a glass globe. This caused the nitrogen and oxygen to react with each other to form nitrogen oxides. These nitrogen oxides dissolved in a solution of an alkali. Large volumes of air were treated in this way and Ramsay always found that about 1% of whatever volume of air he used failed to react.

He named the remaining gas *argon* from the Greek word for 'slow'. He did further experiments of this kind and was able to show that there were other gases in the air as well as nitrogen, oxygen and argon. He went on to discover that air also contained krypton (which means 'hidden'), neon (which means 'new') and xenon (which means 'stranger').

Ramsay was dealing with very tiny amounts of these gases, as Table 1 shows. His experiments must have been very carefully designed and carried out with great precision.

Element	Percentage in air	Date discovered
nitrogen, N	78.09	1772
oxygen, O	20.95	1774
argon, Ar	0.93	1894
neon, Ne	0.0018	1898
krypton, Kr	0.00011	1898
xenon, Xe	0.000009	1898

Table 1 ▲ Percentage composition of dry air

Test Yourself

2   Try to find out the uses of the inert gases argon, neon, krypton and xenon.

Compounds

There are 92 naturally occurring chemical elements known; the names and symbols for some of them are given in Table 2. Remember: the symbol is a shorthand way of representing the element. Elements contain only one kind of atom. There is a full table of these 92 elements in the Periodic Table shown in Figure 2, Chapter 5.

Element	Symbol
aluminium	Al
calcium	Ca
carbon	C
chlorine	Cl
hydrogen	H
magnesium	Mg
nitrogen	N
oxygen	O
potassium	K
sodium	Na
sulphur	S

Table 2 ▲   Some elements and their symbols

We could represent the words 'a mixture of magnesium and sulphur' using symbols as 'Mg + S'. If magnesium and sulphur are mixed together it is easy to separate them again (Figure 3).

- Firstly, you would need to dissolve the sulphur in a suitable solvent.
- Filtering would separate the solid magnesium from the solution.
- The solid sulphur could be recovered by allowing the solvent to evaporate.

However, if the mixture of magnesium and sulphur is heated the mixture changes its appearance and a lot of heat is given out. If we now try to get the magnesium and sulphur back, as described above, it cannot be done. This is because the magnesium and sulphur are not there any more as separate elements. A **chemical reaction** has taken place. We can no longer represent the solid that remains as 'Mg + S' – it is something else.

We can show that magnesium and sulphur have reacted to give a new substance because the properties of the new substance are different from those of both magnesium and sulphur. The new substance contains both magnesium atoms and sulphur atoms, so it is a **compound**.

We could express this reaction in words as follows: 'If a mixture of magnesium and sulphur is heated, they react to give a compound.' Using some symbols, we could write:

Mg + S + heat → compound

The compound that is formed is magnesium sulphide, so we could write:

Mg + S + heat → magnesium sulphide

We can represent magnesium sulphide by its **chemical formula**, which is MgS. There is more on chemical formulae later in this chapter (see page 76).

We can now write a chemical equation for the reaction between magnesium and sulphur:

Mg + S → MgS

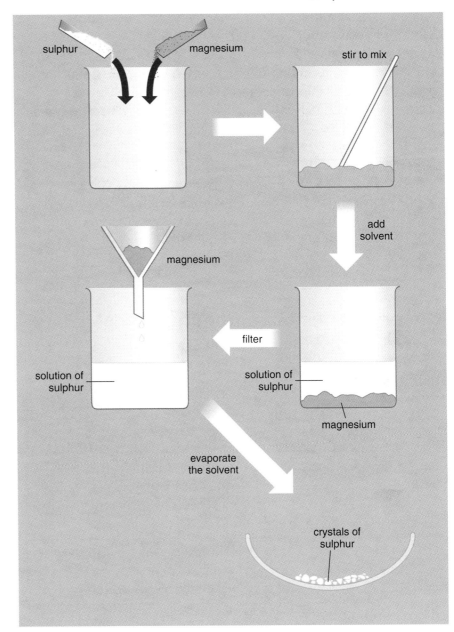

Figure 3 ▲ Separating magnesium and sulphur

Figure 4 ▼ The reaction between magnesium and sulphur

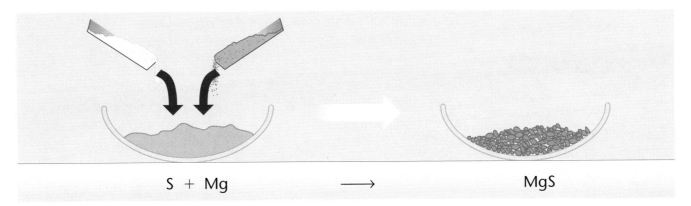

Magnesium and sulphur are the reactants (the substances that react) and magnesium sulphide is the product (the substance formed in the reaction). The arrow '→' means 'reacts to give'. Note that 'heat' has been left out – only the reactants and products are shown in the equation. Heating and other instructions which need to be followed to make a reaction take place are called the reaction conditions.

Test Yourself

3   Write down the symbol equivalents for the following:
    a) a mixture of carbon and sulphur
    b) a mixture of calcium and aluminium.

4   List the differences between an element and a compound.

The properties of compounds

The physical and chemical properties of a compound are different from those of the elements that reacted to make the compound. Table 3 illustrates this.

Compound	Properties	Prepared from
water, H_2O	• colourless liquid • does not burn • not needed for combustion	hydrogen, H_2 – burns easily, colourless gas oxygen, O_2 – needed for combustion, colourless gas
ammonia, NH_3	• colourless gas • pungent smell • very soluble in water	nitrogen, N_2, and hydrogen, H_2 – both have no smell and are not very soluble in water
magnesium chloride, $MgCl_2$	• white solid • soluble in water	magnesium, Mg – silvery metal chlorine, Cl_2 – green gas
sulphur dioxide, SO_2	• colourless gas • choking smell • very soluble in water	sulphur, S – yellow solid, insoluble in water oxygen, O_2 – colourless gas, no smell, not very soluble in water
calcium oxide, CaO	• white solid • reacts with water to give an alkaline solution	calcium, Ca – silvery metal, reacts with water to form hydrogen oxygen, O_2 – colourless gas

Table 3 ▲   The properties of some compounds, compared with the properties of the elements from which they are formed

5 For each of the following compounds, compare the properties of the elements from which each is formed, with the properties of the compounds.
   a) Hydrogen chloride, HCl – choking, colourless gas which dissolves in water to give an acidic solution.
   b) Nitrogen dioxide, NO_2 – pungent, brown gas, soluble in water to give an acidic solution.
   c) Sulphur dichloride, SCl_2 – smelly, red liquid.

Molecules

When atoms join together in small groups to form a compound, the small groups are called **molecules**. The atoms in these molecules are held together by **chemical bonds**. We can represent the chemical bonds between atoms that are joined together as lines. Figure 5 shows some molecules and the chemical bonds they contain.

When molecules react the chemical bonds within them break, and the atoms make new bonds to form the products.

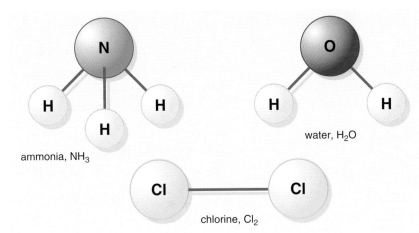

ammonia, NH_3

water, H_2O

chlorine, Cl_2

Figure 5 ▲ 'Ball and stick' diagrams of ammonia, water and chlorine

6 What is meant by the term 'molecule'?

7 Draw 'ball and stick' diagrams of the following molecules:
   a) nitrogen dioxide (NO_2)
   b) sulphur trioxide (SO_3)
   c) tetrachloromethane (CCl_4)
   d) chlorine (Cl_2)
   e) chlorine trifluoride (ClF_3)
   f) hydrogen sulphide (H_2S).

The composition of compounds and mixtures

A compound always contains the same elements in the same fixed proportions. The formula of a compound is always the same, no matter how it is made. For example, magnesium oxide always has the formula MgO – whether it is made by burning magnesium in oxygen or by heating magnesium carbonate.

$$2Mg + O_2 \rightarrow 2MgO$$
$$MgCO_3 \rightarrow MgO + CO_2$$

Note that the '2' in front of MgO in the first equation does not affect the formula – there is still one Mg atom to each O atom in magnesium oxide.

On the other hand, mixtures can have any composition, depending on how much of each substance is added to the mixture.

This is a very important difference between compounds and mixtures, and leads on to ways in which compounds and mixtures can be distinguished.

Melting and boiling points of elements and pure compounds

Although some substances are decomposed by heat, most substances melt when heated. Heating causes the particles in the substance to vibrate increasingly violently until eventually the forces holding the particles together can be overcome and the solid melts to form a liquid. If you continue heating the liquid, you will eventually provide enough energy for the particles to separate sufficiently to move apart. The substances boils and forms a gas. Melting and boiling are discussed in Chapter 1.

Because elements contain only one kind of atom, the forces holding the atoms together are always of the same strength, so a particular element will melt at a specific temperature. Once a liquid has been formed, the forces between all the atoms in it are also of the same strength, so elements also boil at specific temperatures. The melting and boiling points of some elements are shown in Table 4.

Compounds are made of atoms joined together. The atoms are joined together by strong forces, so they stay joined together when the compound melts or boils. Pure compounds are made of only one type of molecule. Because the forces between the molecules that make the compounds are all the same, pure compounds melt and boil at specific temperatures. In this respect, pure compounds behave in the same way as elements.

Element name	Symbol	Melting point in °C	Boiling point in °C
oxygen	O	−218	−183
mercury	Hg	−39	357
bromine	Br	−7	59
potassium	K	68	774
sodium	Na	98	890
sulphur	S	113	445
magnesium	Mg	650	1110
iron	Fe	1535	5300

Table 4 ▲   The melting and boiling points of some elements

The melting and boiling points of some pure compounds are shown in Table 5.

Compound name	Formula	Melting point in °C	Boiling point in °C
methane	CH_4	−182	−161
ammonia	NH_3	−78	−33
sulphur dioxide	SO_2	−73	−10
water	H_2O	0	100
potassium hydroxide	KOH	360	1327
sodium chloride	NaCl	801	1465
magnesium oxide	MgO	2800	3600

Table 5 ▲   Melting and boiling points for some pure compounds

Test Yourself

8   Explain why elements and pure substances always melt at the same temperature.

The melting and boiling points of mixtures

Pure water melts at 0 °C and boils at 100 °C. If some sodium chloride is dissolved in the water it will freeze at a temperature lower than 0 °C and will boil at a temperature above 100 °C. Adding more sodium chloride to a solution lowers the melting point further and raises the boiling point further.

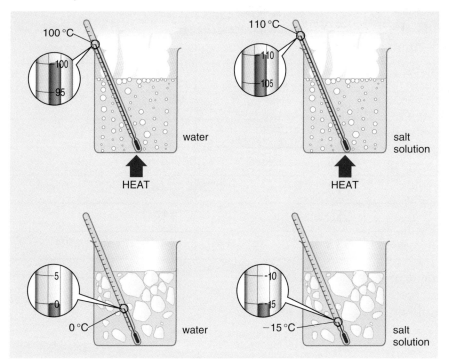

Figure 6 ▲   Dissolved salts lower the freezing point and raise the boiling point of water

Mixtures do not freeze and boil at a particular temperature, but at a temperature that depends on what is in the mixture.

Purity

Some mixtures we buy are described as being 'pure', like some types of food such as orange juice.

Figure 7 ▲

The orange juice is described as 'pure' to show that nothing extra has been added to it during its manufacture. However, the orange juice is really a mixture of many different compounds.

Purity and the scientist

Scientists call something **pure** if it contains only one substance. The label in Figure 8 comes from a container of a laboratory chemical. You can see from the label that the substance is very nearly 100% sodium chloride.

Sodium Chloride Pure

NaCI	
M.W.58.44	
Assay	99.5%
Loss on drying at 105°c	1%
Sulphate (SO₄)	0.02%
Ammonia (NH₃)	0.002%
Iron (Fe)	0.002%
Lead (Pb)	0.0005%
Potassium (K)	0.02%
Description: White crystals.	

Figure 8 ▲ Analysis data from the label on laboratory sodium chloride

It is very difficult to get something 100% pure. Often the small amounts of impurities do not affect the properties of the substance, so it isn't worth the expense of removing the last traces. Scientists use several methods of purification to remove impurities.

Test Yourself

9   What is the difference in the meaning of 'pure' when applied to a chemical and to a glass of fruit juice?

Differences between mixtures and pure substances

- A pure substance has a fixed composition but a mixture can have any composition.
- The substances in a mixture can be separated without the need to do any chemical reactions. We say they can be separated by physical means, such a filtration.
- To break a pure substance down into the elements that make it up we need to carry out some chemical reactions.
- The properties of what goes into a mixture remain the same in the mixture itself, for example lemon juice mixed with water still tastes sour.
- The properties of a pure substance are different from the substances from which it is made. For example, hydrogen (a flammable gas) reacts with oxygen (a gas in which things burn easily) to give water. Water is a liquid that does not burn nor allow things to burn in it.

Equations

You found out about word equations in Chapter 2 (page 16). In Chapter 5 (page 57) you found out about the symbols that are used to represent the different elements.

You can use the element symbols to represented the composition of molecules – this is the chemical formula of the molecule. The chemical formula shows how many of each kind of atom the molecule contains. Instead of writing down the name of a compound, its chemical formula can be used instead. For example, the formula for magnesium sulphide is MgS. The formula tells you:

- what atoms are contained in the compound
- how many atoms of each element are in the compound.

In MgS there is one magnesium atom for every sulphur atom. There are billions and billions of magnesium and sulphur atoms in every gram of magnesium sulphide. However, the formula tells us that for all the atoms you have, every magnesium atom is bonded to a sulphur atom. The magnesium atoms and the sulphur atoms in magnesium sulphide are chemically combined.

Some examples of chemical formulae are given in Table 6. In these formulae, the subscript numbers are important. The number applies to the element symbol immediately before it. For example, the '2' in $CaCl_2$ means that for every calcium atom there are two chlorine atoms.

Name	Formula	Atoms present
aluminium sulphide	Al_2S_3	2 aluminium and 3 sulphur
calcium chloride	$CaCl_2$	1 calcium and 2 chlorine
magnesium oxide	MgO	1 magnesium and 1 oxygen
methane	CH_4	1 carbon and 4 hydrogen
potassium hydroxide	KOH	1 potassium, 1 oxygen and 1 hydrogen
sulphuric acid	H_2SO_4	2 hydrogen, 1 sulphur and 4 oxygen
water	H_2O	2 hydrogen and 1 oxygen

Table 6 ▲

Some chemical formulae appear to be even more complicated than those above – they involve brackets ( ). An example is calcium hydroxide, which has the formula $Ca(OH)_2$. The subscript number after the bracket means that there are two 'OH' groups for every calcium atom. So, calcium hydroxide contains one calcium atom, two oxygen atoms and two hydrogen atoms.

Test Yourself

10 What does the chemical formula of a compound tell you?

Extension box

Writing and balancing chemical equations

Symbol equations are another way of writing down what happens in a reaction. Instead of writing out the full names of all of the reactants and products, scientists use just their chemical formulae. By writing symbol equations, it means that scientists all around the world can understand what is happening in the reaction, as the symbols used are universal.

When writing symbol equations, it is important that the equations are **balanced**. Balancing an equation means making sure that the numbers of atoms of a given element in an equation are the same on both sides of that equation.

Steps in balancing an equation

1 Write down the word equation for the reaction:
hydrochloric + magnesium → magnesium + water
acid   oxide   chloride

2 Replace the words with the correct chemical formula:
$$HCl + MgO \rightarrow MgCl_2 + H_2O$$

Extension box continued

3 Look at both sides of the equation and find an element which isn't balanced.

$HCl + MgO \rightarrow MgCl_2 + H_2O$

$1 \times H$	$2 \times H$
$1 \times Cl$	$2 \times Cl$
$1 \times Mg$	$1 \times Mg$
$1 \times O$	$1 \times O$

The first unbalanced element in our equation is H. We can attempt to balance the H by adding a '2' *in front* of the HCl.

$\mathbf{2}HCl + MgO \rightarrow MgCl_2 + H_2O$

$2 \times H$	$2 \times H$
$2 \times Cl$	$2 \times Cl$
$1 \times Mg$	$1 \times Mg$
$1 \times O$	$1 \times O$

This equation is now balanced.

Remember: you must never change the chemical formula of something in order to balance an equation.

If you really want to do a complete job, you can add **state symbols**. These show whether the substances in the reaction are in the form of solids, liquids, gases or aqueous solutions (i.e. dissolved in water). The different symbols are:

- (s) for solid
- (l) for liquid.
- (g) for gas
- (aq) for aqueous solution

The complete equation then becomes:

$2HCl(aq) + MgO(s) \rightarrow MgCl_2(aq) + H_2O(l)$

Test Yourself

11 Balance the following equations:
a) $CuO + HNO_3 \rightarrow Cu(NO_3)_2 + H_2O$
b) $Na + O_2 \rightarrow Na_2O$
c) $C_3H_8 + O_2 \rightarrow CO_2 + H_2O$
d) $Al_2O_3 + H_2SO_4 \rightarrow Al(SO_4)_3 + H_2O$
e) $CuSO_4 + NaOH \rightarrow Cu(OH)_2 + Na_2SO_4$
f) $Ca(NO_3)_2 \rightarrow CaO + NO_2 + O_2$

Summary

When you have finished studying this chapter, you should understand that:

✔ Mixtures can have a range of compositions.

✔ The substances in a mixture can be separated by physical means.

✔ Mixtures cannot be represented by a chemical formula.

✔ Elements contain only one kind of atom.

✔ Compounds contain more than one kind of atom joined together.

✔ Compounds can be represented by a chemical formula.

✔ The elements in a compound are chemically combined.

✔ The properties of a compound are different from the elements that reacted to form it.

✔ A compound always contains the same elements in fixed proportions.

✔ Pure compounds have fixed melting and boiling points.

✔ Mixtures have variable melting and boiling points.

✔ 'Purity' is a precise chemical term: something is pure if it contains only one substance.

✔ The chemical formula of a compound shows what elements are present.

✔ The chemical formula of a compound shows the relative numbers of the atoms present.

✔ Chemical reactions can be represented using chemical formulae in symbol equations.

End-of-Chapter Questions

1   Explain in your own words the following key terms you have met in this chapter:

mixture

chemical reaction

compound

chemical formula

molecule

chemical bond

pure

balanced

state symbol

2   Harry did some experiments with air to find out how much oxygen and nitrogen his sample of air contained.

He set up the apparatus shown below so he could pass air from syringe A backwards and forwards over the hot copper powder. He did this several times and then pushed all the gas back into syringe A again. The gas had a volume of 100 cm³ at the beginning of the experiment and a volume of 80 cm³ at the end of the experiment.

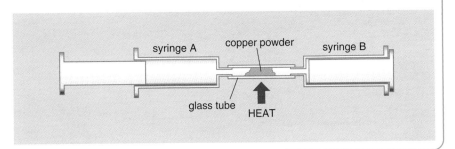

End-of-Chapter Questions continued

a) Why do you think Harry used copper powder, rather than a single lump of copper?

b) i) What gas in the air reacted with the copper? Explain your answer.

ii) What percentage of the air was made up of this gas?

iii) What could Harry have done to ensure that all of this gas had reacted with the copper?

3 How many atoms of the different elements are present in the following compounds?

a) benzene, C_6H_6

b) ethanol, C_2H_5OH

c) sucrose $C_{12}H_{22}O_{11}$

d) hexane, C_6H_{14}

e) calcium nitrate, $Ca(NO_3)_2$

f) ammonium sulphate $(NH_4)_2SO_4$

g) phosphoric acid H_3PO_4

h) calcium hydrogencarbonate, $Ca(HCO_3)_2$

4 Five members of a class were investigating how iron and sulphur react. The equation is:

$$Fe + S \rightarrow FeS$$

The experiments they did are described below.

A Heat mixture of iron and sulphur and allow to cool.

B Powder the product of the reaction and add the mixture to a solvent to dissolve any sulphur remaining and filter.

C Dry the residue on the filter paper and weigh it.

The results of the experiment are shown in the table below.

a) What conclusion can you draw from these figures?

b) i) Plot a graph of mass of iron used (on the horizontal axis) against mass of iron sulphide formed (on the vertical axis).

ii) What conclusion can you draw from this graph?

c) Complete the results table below.

	Jack	Lucy	Emma	Phil	Jane
Mass of iron used in g	3.60	2.96	4.55	1.44	2.10
Mass of iron sulphide formed in g	5.65	4.65	7.14	2.26	3.30
Mass of sulphur in g which reacted with the iron					
Mass of sulphur which reacted with 1 g of iron					

End-of-Chapter Questions continued

i)   Suggest why the figures in the last row of this table are not exactly the same.

ii) How do these results indicate that iron sulphide is a compound, not a mixture?

d) i)   What mass of sulphur would you mix with 4.00 g of iron to ensure that only iron sulphide was formed, with no sulphur left over?

ii) What mass of iron sulphide would be formed when they reacted?

5   Different masses of sodium chloride were dissolved in 100 cm^3 of water and the boiling points of the resulting solutions were measured. The results are shown in the table.

Mass of sodium chloride dissolved in g	Boiling point of the solution in °C
2.30	100.20
4.00	100.35
5.70	100.50
6.80	100.60
8.50	100.75

a) What do the results illustrate about the boiling points of mixtures?

b) i)   Plot a graph of mass of sodium chloride dissolved (on the horizontal axis) against boiling point of the solution (on the vertical axis). How does the boiling point of the solution depend on the mass of sodium chloride dissolved in the water?

ii) Use your graph to obtain a value for the boiling point of pure water.

c) What mass of salt would have to be added to 100 cm^3 of water to give a solution that boiled at 102.0 °C?

7

Rocks and weathering

If you visit the same beach regularly, do you notice differences each time you go? Perhaps the pebbles on the beach and the way the sand is piled up changes from year to year?

You may even find that a large rock has been broken into smaller pieces, that part of a cliff has collapsed or that a new mud bank has appeared.

This is Marsden Rock in Northumberland. In 1986 the rock arch fell down. The stone pillar that was left was blown up because it had become unstable. So Marsden Rock now looks very different.

The rocks on the surface of the Earth are constantly being broken down and worn away. This gives rise to very spectacular rock formations, such as those in the picture above. The process through which rocks are broken down is called **weathering.** The breaking down and movement of rock is called **erosion**. The rocks on the beach and cliff face are constantly being weathered and eroded by the sea. It is difficult to imagine that water can break down rock because rocks seem so hard. But let's take a closer look at rocks to find out what they are made of.

What are rocks made of?

If you examine a sample of rock you will see that it is made up of lots of smaller particles called **grains**.

Figure 1 ▲ a) Granite and b) sandstone

These grains may be of different sizes and colours. The grains are made up of different **minerals**, which are, in turn, made of a number of different substances. For example, sandstone is made up of quartz, which is silicon dioxide. Granite contains a lot of feldspar, which is potassium aluminium silicate. Limestone is made up of calcite, which is calcium carbonate. Pyrite is a shiny mineral made up of iron sulphide. It is often mistaken for gold and has been nicknamed, 'fools' gold'. The green colour of malachite is caused by copper carbonate.

Figure 2 ▲ a) Quartz b) pyrite c) calcite d) malachite and e) feldspar

Each rock is made up of different types and amounts of minerals such as these.

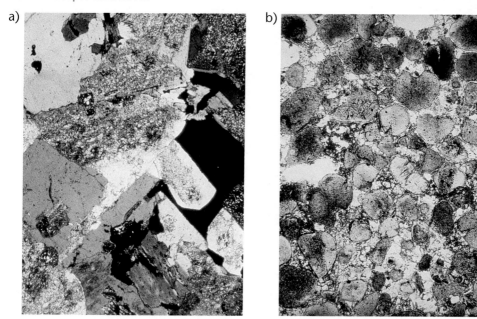

Figure 3 ▲ a) Granite and b) sandstone

You can get a better idea of what the grains in a sample of rock look like by using a magnifying glass to examine them. Figure 3 shows the grains in granite and sandstone, both magnified 20 times.

Types of rock

Rocks can be divided into three main groups:

1 Igneous
2 Sedimentary
3 Metamorphic

Each of these groups of rock has been formed in a different way and, as a result, each group has different properties.

- Igneous rocks are formed from molten rock inside the Earth, which cools and solidifies.
- Granite is an igneous rock.
- Sedimentary rocks are formed when water deposits layers of pebbles, sand and mud.
- Sandstone is a sedimentary rock
- Metamorphic rocks are formed inside the Earth as a result of extreme heat and pressure.
- Marble is a metamorphic rock.
- The different types of rock are connected through the rock cycle (see Chapter 8).

Test Yourself

1   a) What are the grains in rocks made of?
    b) Why do they sometimes look different from one another?

2   Name a rock that has large grains in it.

3   Name the three main groups of rock.

How do the grains fit together?

The grains in samples of granite and sandstone appear to be tightly packed together, but if we put a piece of each type of rock in water, we will see a difference.

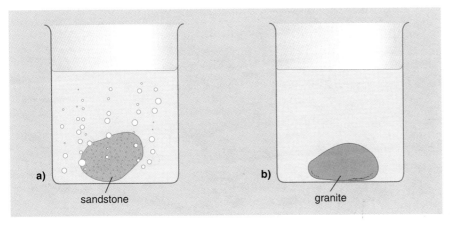

a) sandstone
b) granite

Figure 4 ▲   Air can get into sandstone but not into granite

When you place a sample of sandstone in water, bubbles of air rise to the surface of the water. The grains in sandstone do not fit tightly together and air gets into the spaces between the grains. It is this air that bubbles out when we put the rock in water. The grains in granite are interlocking and there are no spaces between them and no air gets in. As a result, we do not see bubbles rising from the granite when we put it in water.

We say that sandstone is a **porous** rock – air and water can get into the gaps between the grains. Granite is **non-porous**. Limestone is another kind of sedimentary rock. It is less porous than sandstone, but more porous than granite. These results are summarised in Table 1.

Rock	How porous is it?	How do the grains fit together?
granite	rock becomes more porous ↓	grains fit less tightly together ↓
limestone		
sandstone		

Table 1 ▲

It is easy to show that sandstone is porous. If you weigh a piece of sandstone before you place it in water and after, you will record an increase in mass. The increase in mass is due to the water entering the spaces between the grains. If you repeated the experiment with granite, there would be no increase in mass.

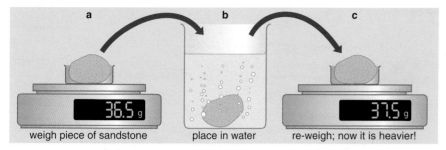

a   b   c

36.5 g   37.5 g

weigh piece of sandstone   place in water   re-weigh; now it is heavier!

Figure 5 ▲   Water fills the gaps between the grains in the sandstone

Water can penetrate porous rock but will not penetrate non-porous rock. That is why sedimentary rocks, such as sandstone, tend to weather faster than igneous rocks, such as granite.

When the water from a layer of a porous rock meets a layer of non-porous rock the results can be dramatic. Figure 6 shows the River Loue – the river seems to come from nowhere and suddenly appears out of the rock. Water has percolated through the porous rock until it met a layer of non-porous rock. The water then ran along the top of the non-porous rock layer, suddenly bursting through the cliff face. Notice the layers of different sedimentary rocks in this picture. Each of these layers was deposited slowly over millions of years.

Figure 6 ◄   River Loue, France

Test Yourself

4   The table below shows the masses of two samples of rock before and after putting them in water.

	Rock A	Rock B
Mass after putting rock in water	126 g	146 g
Mass before putting rock in water	125 g	133 g

a) Which rock is more porous?

b) Explain why putting the rocks in water leads to an increase in mass.

Weathering of rock

a)
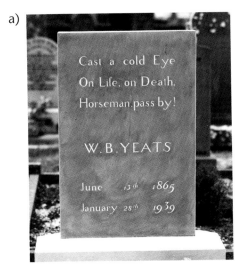

b)

Figure 7 ▲   a) This gravestone is still quite new, you can still read the inscription. b) This gravestone has been eroded by acid rain, none of the words are visible any more.

Old stone items often show their age by looking more worn than newer items. For example, the lettering on gravestones becomes less clear and old carvings can sometimes be hard to recognise as anything in particular. These changes are due to weathering.

Weathering is the name given to any process which breaks a rock down into smaller pieces or dissolves it away.

Weathering can be divided into two main types.

- **Physical weathering** is caused by water, wind or by the heating and cooling of the rock.
- **Chemical weathering** is when water dissolves substances in the rock and carries them away in solution.

Some rocks contain only one mineral and if this mineral dissolves easily in water then the rock may eventually disappear completely. It is more common for only *some* of the minerals in a rock to dissolve. If this happens, then the rock crumbles as the minerals holding the grains together in it are dissolved away.

Chemical weathering

Rainwater contains carbon dioxide, dissolved from the atmosphere, which makes it acidic. The acid in rainwater reacts with minerals in rock, causing them to dissolve and the rock to weather.

During the dissolving process chemical reactions take place. Limestone weathers rapidly because it is made of calcium carbonate, which reacts easily with acids. Many old buildings were built of limestone rocks. Some of these buildings have been badly damaged by weathering.

limestone + hydrochloric acid → calcium chloride + carbon dioxide + water
$$CaCO_3 + 2HCl \rightarrow CaCl_2 + CO_2 + H_2O$$

More recently, the burning of fossil fuels has increased the amount sulphur dioxide in the atmosphere, and this has increased the acidity of rainwater. Commonly called 'acid rain', this has caused many limestone statues and buildings to wear away rapidly, especially in industrial areas where there has been a lot of atmospheric pollution.

Not all rocks dissolve equally easily in rainwater because the minerals in them differ in solubility.

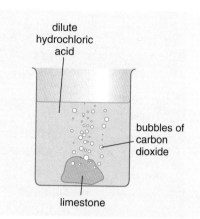

Figure 8 ▲ Limestone reacting with hydrochloric acid

Test Yourself

5   Examine as many examples of rock as you can near where you live and describe the changes that have been caused by weathering.

6   Name one rock which is weathered easily by chemicals. Why does this rock weather easily?

7   Explain why adding hydrochloric acid to limestone is not likely to represent accurately how the rock might weather in the rain.

Limestone is made of one mineral, calcium carbonate, but granite contains many more. The minerals present in a sample of granite weather at different rates. The minerals in granite and how they weather are shown in Table 2.

Quartz is chemically the same as sand and occurs as large crystals in granite. Mica is found as very thin crystals; it is the mica that gives granite its glittery appearance.

The feldspar in granite acts rather like glue, holding the other minerals together. When the feldspar is weathered out of the granite, the other minerals are left as individual crystals and then continue to weather on their own, much more slowly. The feldspar also assists in the break-up of the granite by swelling during weathering, forcing the other minerals apart. When granite weathers, the final result is mainly quartz crystals because all the other minerals dissolve away or are washed away.

Notice the difference between the weathering of limestone and the weathering of granite. Limestone eventually dissolves completely during weathering. In granite one mineral is weathered selectively, leading to the disintegration of the granite.

Figure 9 ▲ Acid rain has worn away this statue

Mineral	Rate of weathering	Products of weathering
feldspar	weathers much more rapidly than the other minerals in granite	clay + other substances in solution
iron/magnesium minerals	both weather more slowly than feldspar, but more quickly than quartz	clay + iron oxides + other substances in solution
mica		clay + iron oxides + other substances in solution
quartz	does not weather	none

Table 2 ▲ Weathering of the minerals found in granite

a)

b)

Figure 10 ▲ a) A freshly cut piece of granite and b) granite which has been weathered – the feldspar has been removed before the other minerals

Test Yourself

8   How does the chemical weathering of granite differ from the chemical weathering of limestone?

The chemical weathering of rocks dissolves some of the substances in the rock. All natural water has salts of various kinds dissolved in it. When water that has been involved in the weathering of rock evaporates, the dissolved salts are deposited as solid sediments. The minerals deposited most commonly in this way are halite (sodium chloride) and gypsum (calcium sulphate). This leads to huge salt flats, such as these in Utah, USA.

Physical weathering

Freeze-thaw

Water is an important agent in physical weathering. No chemical reactions take place in physical weathering; the rock is broken into smaller pieces by the action of wind or water, for example the freezing of water in cracks in the rock.

Water can enter a small crack in a piece of rock. Water expands on freezing. The force created as the water expands pushes the sides of the crack apart, making the crack wider. The ice thaws and more water can then enter the widened crack and this water can freeze too. Eventually the rock splits. This is called the **freeze-thaw process** and it takes place over a long period.

Figure 11 ▲ Salt Flats, Utah

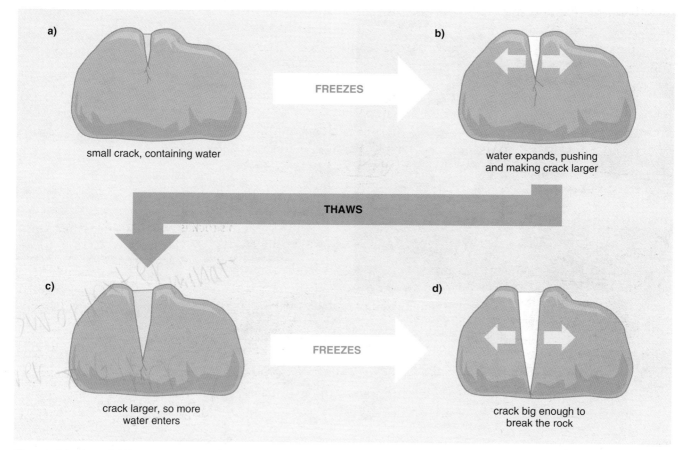

a)

small crack, containing water

FREEZES

b)

water expands, pushing and making crack larger

THAWS

c)

crack larger, so more water enters

FREEZES

d)

crack big enough to break the rock

Figure 12 ▲ a) Water enters cracks in the rock. b) When the temperature drops, the water freezes and expands, causing the crack in the rock to enlarge. c) The water in the rock thaws. This process is repeated over many years. d) Eventually the crack is enlarged so much that the rock breaks apart

In many mountainous regions there are large scree slopes made from fragments of rock shattered by the freezing of water in cracks on the rock face. The fragments are often angular and quite sharp because the rock splits in straight lines.

Weathering due to the freezing of water is most effective in countries such as Britain, where the overnight temperature is regularly below 0 °C at night but fairly warm during the day. The water melts during the day and then freezes the next time the temperature reaches 0 °C. Weathering due to freezing is not very important in very cold countries because the water simply stays frozen all of the time.

Figure 13 ▲   A scree slope

Heating and cooling

All substances expand when they are heated, because the particles in them vibrate more violently and take up more space. Some of the minerals in a piece of rock expand more than others. This causes a strain in the rock which can cause the rock to crack and eventually to break up.

You can demonstrate weathering due to heating and cooling by the experiment shown in Figure 14. Weathering due to heating and cooling is most effective where the daytime temperatures are high and those at night are low. Conditions like these are often found in deserts or on high mountains.

Figure 15 ▼   This rock is being weathered by heating and cooling

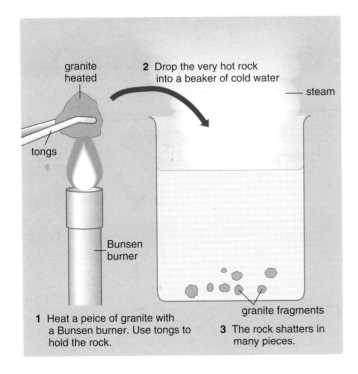

granite heated

2 Drop the very hot rock into a beaker of cold water

— steam

tongs

Bunsen burner

granite fragments

1 Heat a peice of granite with a Bunsen burner. Use tongs to hold the rock.

3 The rock shatters in many pieces.

Figure 14 ◄   Experiment to show weathering due to heating and cooling

Test Yourself

9 The table below shows the daily maximum and minimum temperatures for four locations.

	Maximum temperature in °C	Minimum temperature in °C
location A	40	5
location B	28	14
location C	20	9
location D	15	−5

a) In which location(s) might you expect to find rocks weathered by heating and cooling? Explain your answer.

b) In which location(s) might you expect to find rocks weathered by the freeze-thaw cycle of water? Explain your answer.

Wind

Wind is an important weathering agent, particularly of soft rocks such as sandstone. The wind carries small rock fragments which act as an abrasive, similar to sandpaper, to weather the rock.

Weathering by soil and plants

It is quite common to turn over a piece of rock lying on the ground and to find that the underside is more weathered than the upper surface. This is partly because the underside of the rock is kept wetter than the upper surface, but also because some organic matter in the soil is converted to humic acids. These acids increase the rate of chemical weathering.

Figure 16 ▲   These sandstone rocks have been eroded by the wind

Plant roots also assist physical weathering by growing into cracks in the rock and widening them. Bits of rock will break off and also the enlarged cracks make it easier for water to penetrate the rock.

Observing weathering

Weathering is a very gradual process. It is much easier to follow weathering by using **time-lapse photography**. In time-lapse photography, a series of pictures is taken each day over a long period of time. These photos are then shown quickly one after the other. This gives the appearance that very slow events have been speeded up. Time-lapse photography is used more and more by scientists to follow slow changes.

Transport of weathered rock

The weathering processes described above have the effect of reducing the size of rock particles. When the particles become small enough they can be carried away from the place they were formed – they can be **transported** – by wind or water.

Transport by water currents can take several forms, depending on the size of the rock particles, as shown in Table 3. The dimensions shown are estimates; the sizes of particles can vary outside these limits.

Size of rock particles	How transported?
large, 10–60 mm in diameter	by rolling along the bed of the river
medium, 2–10 mm in diameter	by rolling along the bed of the river or by bouncing along it
small, up to 2 mm in diameter	by bouncing along the bed of the river or carried in suspension
very small, less than 0.1 mm in diameter	carried in suspension

Table 3 ▲ Transportation of rock particles by water

Particles classified as 'large' or 'medium' in Table 3 can only be transported by water currents that flow quickly. Very often this is only in rivers and streams in mountainous areas and in other places after heavy rainfall.

Most of the particles carried by water are very small and are called **sediments** – it is the very fine sediment, called silt, that is responsible for the muddy appearance of many rivers. Sediments are carried along suspended in the water as long as the water is moving quickly enough. If the water slows down, even the smallest particles of sediment will settle to the bottom. The slowing of the water leads to **deposition** of the sediment on the bed of the river or stream.

Test Yourself

10 Explain the difference between *weathering* and *erosion*.

11 Copy the diagram below and mark on it where you think sediment will be deposited. You should be able to explain your answer.

Figure 17 ▲

The most obvious examples of deposited sediments are to be seen where a river reaches the sea. The river slows down so suddenly that almost all of the sediment it is carrying is deposited. The result is a river delta. The deposited sediments are often very fertile and river deltas can be important for agricultural purposes.

As particles are transported they rub against each other and against the bed of the river or stream. This has two effects:

- the particles become smaller
- the particles become rounder and smoother.

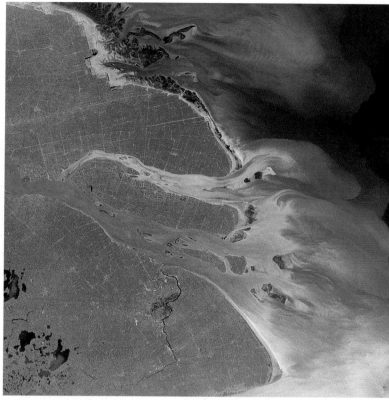

Figure 18 ▲ The delta at the mouth of the River Yangtze in China. The swirls of blue and beige are sediment

The distance a particle can be carried by water currents depends on the mass of the particle and also its size. Larger particles are carried shorter distances than smaller particles. Particles of the same size tend to be found in the same place in a river or stream – the particles have been **sorted by size** along the course of a river.

When a water current slows down, there is not enough energy to carry the suspended sediment and it sinks to the bottom. Large particles sink more rapidly than small ones, so sediments are also sorted by size, with the largest particles at the bottom of the river bed and the smallest at the top.

The characteristic layers in sediments form as a result of this size sorting and the layers are made more obvious if the various particles have different colours, as they often do.

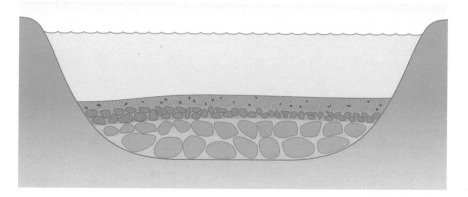

Figure 19 ◄ Weathered material is transported and deposited in layers according to size

Test Yourself

12 Explain why sediment is deposited when a current of water slows down.

Sediments that were once alive

So far, the sediments we have considered have been made up of very small rock fragments, formed by weathering. Not all sediments are made up of rock fragments – some of the largest sediments are made of the remains of dead organisms.

Millions of years ago the seas were full of tiny marine creatures. These creatures used the minerals in the sea to build primitive skeletons and when they died the remains of the skeletons sank to the sea bed as sediments. These animal remains are known as **fossils**. Chalk and limestone were formed in this way and deposits hundreds of metres in thickness were created.

The skeletons in some sediments are large enough to see with the naked eye.

Fossils can be useful in dating rocks. Two pieces of rock found in different places but with the same fossils in them are likely to be of a similar age.

Fossils can also be used to show that a piece of rock was once part of a larger piece, from which it has been broken. This can be done even if the broken fragment has been transported some distance.

Figure 20 ▲ Beachy Head is made of chalk

Figure 21 ► The fossils are easily visible in this limestone

Because sediments are formed by particles settling in water, they form a series of parallel layers. The fossils in the layers provide useful information about what was alive when the layer was being formed. The thickness of the layer can give information about the numbers of marine creatures alive at the time. A thick layer indicates there were lots of creatures alive, perhaps due to a warm period in the Earth's history or to a particularly good supply of food. Thin layers may be associated with harsh weather conditions or a shortage of food.

Extension box

How fossils form

The formation of fossils of bones and teeth begins when animals are buried by sediment very soon after the death of the animal. Gradually, more and more sediment covers the remains. Over a long time, the hard parts of the animal are changed in various ways:

★ the bone decays and water containing dissolved minerals gets into the bones and gradually replaces the bone with minerals

★ spaces in the remains left by rotting internal organs are filled with minerals in the same way.

Eventually, a copy of the original animal is formed in which the bones and the internal organs have been replaced by minerals – the fossil is an exact copy of the original animal. Some fossils of soft materials, such as skin and wood, have been found, but this is rare because they usually rot too quickly. Scientists estimate that only a very small percentage of dead animals become fossils; most simply rotted away or were eaten by scavengers.

Figure 22 shows the conditions needed for fossils to form.

Figure 22 ▼

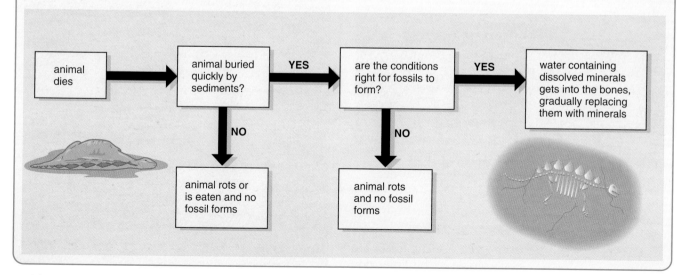

The greatest fossilist the world has ever known

Figure 23 ▲ Mary Anning (1799–1847)

Mary Anning has been called 'the greatest fossilist the world ever knew'. She was born in Lyme Regis, in Dorset. At Lyme Regis the cliffs contain many fossils from the Jurassic period (208 to 146 million years ago). The nineteenth century was the age of the dinosaur hunter. Initially, Mary began collecting fossils as a hobby, but when her father died in 1810 she began to collect fossils to sell, to make a little money.

A famous fossil collector, Thomas Birch, who thought a great deal of Mary's ability, sold his own fossil collection to ensure that Mary could devote more time to the scientific collection and study of fossils. Mary had no formal scientific training, but the following tribute to her by Lady Harriet Sivester in 1824 shows that this did not affect her ability to become an expert in the study of fossils.

'. . . the extraordinary thing in this young woman is that she has made herself so thoroughly acquainted with the science that the moment she finds any bones she knows to what tribe they belong.

She fixes the bones on a frame with cement and then makes drawings and has them engraved . . . It is certainly a wonderful instance of divine favour – that this poor, ignorant girl should be so blessed, for by reading and application she has arrived to that degree of knowledge as to be in the habit of writing and talking with professors and other clever men on the subject, and they all acknowledge that she understands more of the science than anyone else in this kingdom.'

Mary Anning is credited with the discovery of the first ichthyosaur and plesiosaur skeletons. These were two groups of marine reptiles that lived around the same time as the dinosaurs.

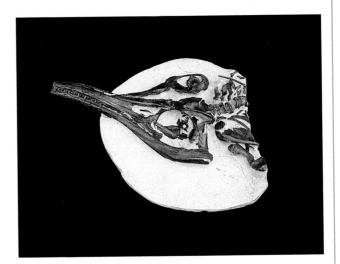

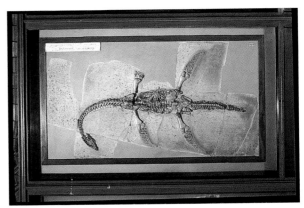

Figure 24 ▲ a) *Ichthyosaurus* and b) *Plesiosaurus*

Summary

When you have finished studying this chapter, you should understand that:

- ✔ Rocks are made up of smaller grains, made of different minerals.

- ✔ The size of the grains affects the texture of the rock.

- ✔ Some rocks allow water between the grains; these rocks are called porous rocks.

- ✔ Rocks are broken down by weathering, which can be chemical or physical.

- ✔ Chemical weathering changes the rock and dissolves parts of it away.

- ✔ Physical weathering is caused by water, wind and by changes in temperature.

- ✔ Weathering is a slow process.

- ✔ Time-lapse photography can make the events of weathering easier to follow.

- ✔ Weathered rock can be transported by water. This is called erosion.

- ✔ Transportation sorts rocks by size and changes their shape and size.

End-of-Chapter Questions

1 Explain in your own words the following key terms you have met in this chapter:

grain

mineral

porous

non-porous

weathering

physical weathering

chemical weathering

time-lapse photography

transported

sediment

deposition

sorted by size

fossils

2 Explain the differences between physical and chemical weathering.

3 Can you suggest why chemical weathering is more rapid where there has also been a lot of physical weathering? (Hint: Think about particle size.)

4 John and Sue designed an experiment to investigate how far rock particles of different sizes would travel in water. They set up a sloping trough to represent a river bed and used a hosepipe to make the water current. They marked the trough at 10 cm intervals along its length.

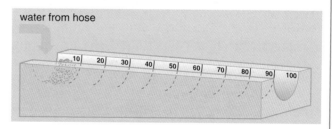

They placed a mixture of rock particles of different sizes at the top of the trough and turned the hosepipe on. After 5 minutes they turned the hosepipe off and measured the sizes of the particles at each 10 cm mark. The table shows their results.

End-of-Chapter Questions continued

Distance in cm	Size of particle in mm
10	18
20	12
30	10
40	8
50	6
60	5
70	4
80	3
90	2
100	2

a) i) Draw a graph of distance (on the horizontal axis) against particle size (on the vertical axis).

ii) Draw a line of best fit through the points.

iii) What can you tell from the graph. How can you explain it?

b) i) The particle size was determined by taking five particles at each distance, measuring the diameter of each and taking an average. Why do you think they did this?

ii) How could they have improved the accuracy of their experiment?

5 Your teacher has given you three samples of different limestone rocks and asked you to find out the relative amounts of calcium carbonate in each. Devise a series of experiments to do this. Your teacher reminded you that calcium carbonate gave carbon dioxide when acid was added to it.

6 Lucy took a large jar of water and put some soil from the garden in it. She shook the jar and then left it to stand for 10 minutes. Here is a drawing of the jar afterwards. Explain why the contents of the jar look the way they do.

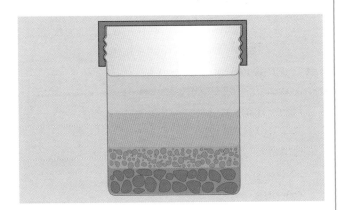

8

The rock cycle

The appearance of the Earth's surface does not seem to change during our lifetime. This is because most of the changes that affect how the Earth looks take place very slowly. Although we may not notice the changes, they are happening all the time. In some parts of the Earth, mountains are gradually being worn away by erosion, elsewhere, mountains are being formed, very slowly. Many of these changes take many millions of years, but some volcanic events are very rapid and usually violent.

New features can be created in a few days or weeks, such as happened when the island of Surtsey was formed. A submarine volcano erupted about 20 miles from Iceland to form the new island, which rose 130 metres from the sea floor between 8 November and 15 November 1963.

Figure 1 ▼ The Island of Surtsey

These changes to the surface of the Earth, the weathering and erosion of rock and the formation of new rocks are part of the **rock cycle.** The rock cycle links the processes of rock formation, weathering and erosion.

Using the rock cycle, we can explain the formation of the three main types of rock:

1 Sedimentary rock
2 Metamorphic rock
3 Igneous rock

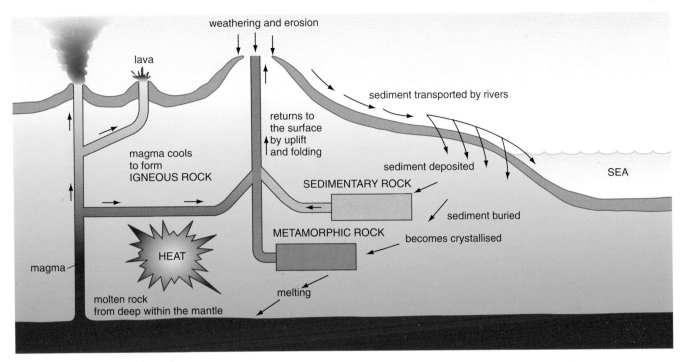

Figure 2 ▲   The rock cycle

From sediment to sedimentary rocks

Rocks are broken down by chemical and physical weathering. The particles of rock, sand and mud are then transported by rivers and streams and deposited as sediment on the bottom of seas and lakes (see page 93, Chapter 7). These sediments are soft, but over many millions of years, as more and more layers are deposited, pressure builds up and squashes the soft sediments so that they turn into hard sedimentary rock.

Figure 3 ◀   It took millions of years for the layers of rock in the Grand Canyon to be deposited

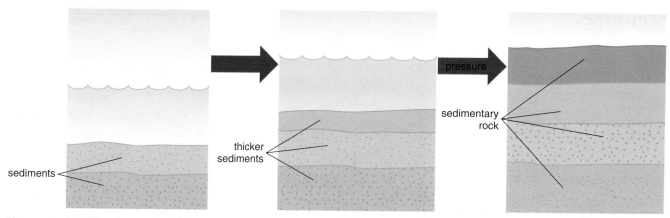

Figure 4 ▲   The formation of sedimentary rock from sediments

Solutions of salts are forced into the gaps between the particles. Solid salts are left behind when the water is later squeezed out under pressure. This process is called **cementation** and it glues the particles of sediment firmly together. The result is sedimentary rock.

You need to be careful not to confuse the terms 'sediment' and 'sedimentary rock'.

Chalk and *limestone* are sedimentary rocks. Chalk is mostly made of the skeletons of marine creatures and is a crumbly rock. Limestone also contains the skeletons of marine creatures but it is formed under greater pressure than chalk. The greater pressure crushes the skeletons and makes limestone harder and denser than chalk.

The main component of limestone and chalk is calcium carbonate, from the shells of the sea creatures. We can tell that calcium carbonate is present because limestone reacts with acid to give carbon dioxide. We can test for carbon dioxide with limewater. Limewater turns milky if carbon dioxide is passed through it (see page 19, Chapter 2). Therefore acid is used by geologists as a test for limestone.

Sandstone is made from grains of sand. The grains are pushed up against each other to form a sedimentary rock, which is crumbly and porous.

Sedimentary rocks often contain fossils. Fossils are formed when dead plant and animal remains are buried by sediment (see page 96, Chapter 7). The shape of the animal and plant remains are often preserved in the rock.

Shale is another kind of sedimentary rock. It is made from compressed particles of clay and mud.

Figure 5 ▲   The outline of this fossilised ginkgo leaf is clearly visible in the rock

Summary

Sedimentary rocks:

- have a layered structure
- are porous
- consist of mineral grains cemented together
- tend to be crumbly.

Metamorphic rocks

As more and more sediments are deposited, sedimentary rocks become buried deep underground where the pressure is very high. As the temperature increases by 30 °C for every kilometre you go below the surface of the Earth, buried sedimentary rocks also tend to become hotter. The sedimentary rock can be changed by this heat and pressure into other kinds of rock. Scientists call rocks formed by the action of heat and pressure on sedimentary rock **metamorphic rocks**. The word 'metamorphic' comes from two Greek words meaning 'changed form'.

The rock that is changed by heat and pressure is called the **parent rock**. The chemicals in the rock are changed. As a result, the parent rock and the metamorphic rock formed from it often look very different.

Parent sedimentary rock	Metamorphic rock
limestone or chalk	marble
shale	slate
sandstone	quartzite

Table 1 ▲

Figure 6 ▼ Limestone a) changes into marble b)

a)
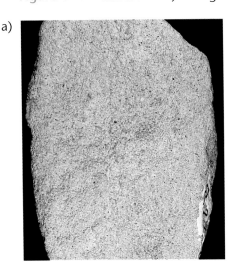

b)

Test Yourself

1 How does a sediment differ from a sedimentary rock?

2 Explain the existence of layers in sedimentary rocks in your own words.

3 Describe a chemical test that could distinguish between sandstone and limestone.

a)
b)

Figure 7 ▲   Sandstone a) changes into quartzite b)

Summary

Sedimentary rocks are changed by heat and pressure to form metamorphic rock. The metamorphic rock is often very different to the sedimentary rock from which it is formed. Metamorphic rocks are often:

- less porous
- harder.

Igneous rocks

Metamorphic and sedimentary rocks get pushed further down into the Earth's crust. We do not know the exact temperature at the centre of the Earth, but it may be close to 5000 °C. If so, this would be about the same temperature as the surface of the Sun. This temperature is high enough to melt all known substances, including rocks.

Under the surface of the Earth there are huge amounts of molten rock, called **magma**. This layer of molten rock is called the mantle. The rock is kept molten by the heat given out when rocks in the Earth give off radioactivity. Often the magma breaks through the crust of the Earth and reaches the surface. When the molten rock reaches the surface, it is called **lava**. Lava usually reaches the surface during volcanic eruptions.

Igneous rocks form whenever magma or lava cools and crystallises. Crystals form because the particles in the molten magma move less quickly and come closer together. Eventually, the forces between the particles make them take up the orderly arrangement we call a crystal.

Test Yourself

4   Name two metamorphic rocks and the parent rocks from which each is formed.

Figure 8 ▲ A sample of granite

Figure 9 ▲ A sample of basalt

If molten magma cools rapidly, crystals start to form at all points in the magma and start to increase in size. Before long, all of the magma has crystallised and it is all solid before the crystals have had time to grow very much.

If the magma cools slowly, the first crystal to form can continue to grow and can become quite large before all the magma has solidified.

Types of igneous rock

There are two types of igneous rock:

- intrusive
- extrusive.

Intrusive igneous rock forms when magma cools slowly deep within the Earth. The slow cooling gives rocks with large crystals, such as *granite*.

Extrusive igneous rock forms when lava cools quickly at the surface of the Earth. The rapid cooling gives rise to rocks with small crystals, such as *basalt*.

If the cooling is very rapid, there is no time for crystals to form. Instead, a **volcanic glass** is formed. The most common volcanic glass is *obsidian*. It is usually black in colour.

Magma contains gases dissolved under pressure. When this pressure is released at the surface, sometimes the gases are trapped as bubbles in the rock. The trapped gas gives these rocks a very low density. *Pumice* is the best-known example of this type of igneous rock – the density of pumice is so low that it floats on water.

Figure 10 ▲ Obsidian

a)

b)

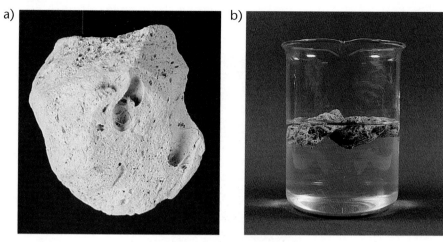

Figure 11 ▲   a) Pumice and b) the density of pumice is so low that it floats on water

Magma is held in magma chambers up to 200 km beneath the Earth. The material of the Earth insulates the magma, rather like a blanket, so cooling is slow. Lava usually reaches the surface of the Earth as a result of volcanic eruptions. Lava cools much more rapidly. Volcanoes also give out large quantities of ash. This ash can be thrown up to heights of many miles and can be transported all round the world by the wind, see Figure 12.

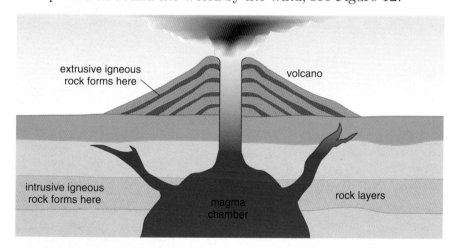

extrusive igneous rock forms here

volcano

intrusive igneous rock forms here

magma chamber

rock layers

Figure 12 ◄

Test Yourself

5   What is the difference between magma and lava?

6   Why are fossils not found in igneous rocks?

7   Draw a picture showing where and how intrusive and extrusive igneous rocks are formed.

8   Explain how the rate of cooling affects the sizes of the crystals in igneous rocks.

Summary

The rate of cooling influences the type of rock formed, as follows:

- slow cooling over thousands to millions of years leads to granite, which has large crystals
- rapid cooling over days to weeks leads to basalt, which has small crystals
- very rapid cooling over hours to days leads to obsidian, which has no crystals.

Igneous rocks that form on the surface of the Earth, as a result of volcanic eruptions, are subject to weathering and erosion. The rock cycle starts again.

Driving the rock cycle

The Earth's surface appears to be fixed, but in fact it is constantly on the move. Most of this movement is so slow that we cannot see it but there are some dramatic cases when the movement of the Earth's surface is very obvious to us. These are earthquakes.

The rock surface of the Earth is called the Earth's crust. At most it is 10 km thick. Underneath the Earth's **crust** is hot, molten rock (magma) at a temperature of 1400 °C. This layer of magma is called the **mantle**. The molten rock in the mantle is moving around, pulling the surface crust with it. At the centre of the Earth is the **core**, which is a ball of very dense hot iron at 4000 °C.

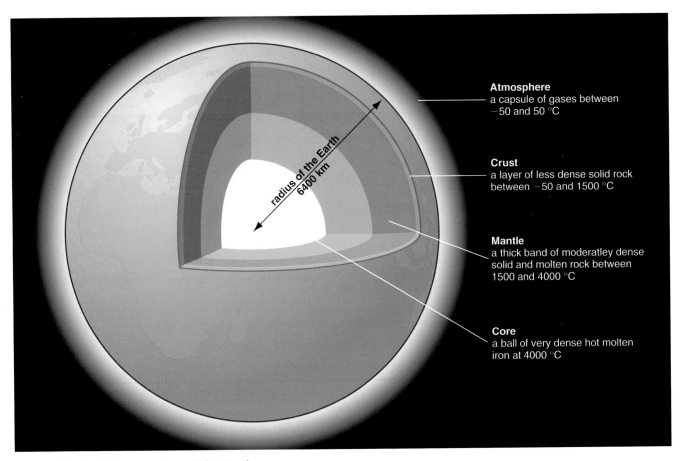

Atmosphere
a capsule of gases between −50 and 50 °C

Crust
a layer of less dense solid rock between −50 and 1500 °C

Mantle
a thick band of moderatley dense solid and molten rock between 1500 and 4000 °C

Core
a ball of very dense hot molten iron at 4000 °C

radius of the Earth 6400 km

Figure 13 ▲ The structure of the Earth

The surface crust is not in one piece, but is split into huge plates, which fit together like a giant jigsaw puzzle (Figure 14). The oceans and continents sit on top of these plates. It is these plates which are moved by the currents of molten rock in the mantle. Where these plates are being pulled together, earthquakes and volcanoes can occur. This theory of the movement of the plates, called **plate tectonics**, has helped us to understand why volcanoes and earthquakes occur.

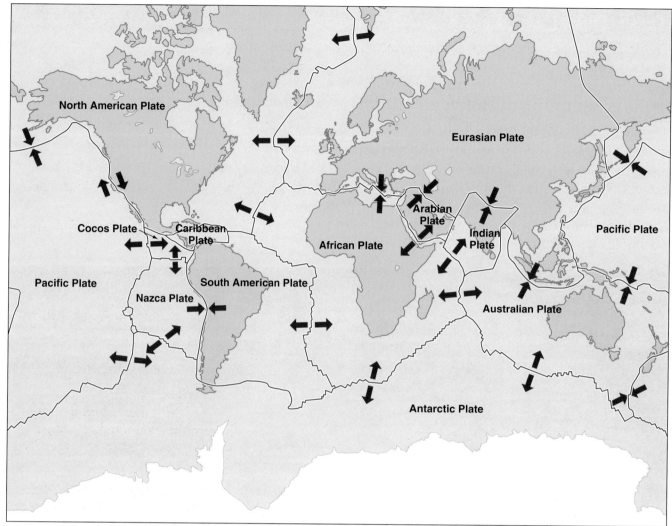

Figure 14 ▲ The surface of the Earth is made up of plates, which are slowly moving

Summary

When you have finished studying this chapter, you should understand that:

✔ Sedimentary rocks are formed from solid particles which settle under water.

✔ Metamorphic rocks are formed by the action of heat and pressure on sedimentary rocks.

✔ Igneous rocks are formed when molten magma cools and solidifies.

✔ Intrusive igneous rocks are formed when magma cools slowly; they have large crystals in them.

✔ Extrusive igneous rocks are formed when magma cools rapidly; they have small crystals in them.

End-of-Chapter Questions

1 Explain in your own words the following key terms you have met in this chapter:

cementation
sedimentary rock
metamorphic rock
parent rock
magma
lava
igneous rock
volcanic glass

2 The diagrams below show the structures of two types of rock.

a) Which rock is sedimentary and which rock is igneous?

b) Explain how you made your choice.

3 The diagrams below show samples of granite and basalt.

 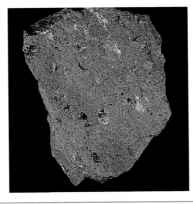

a) Which rock sample is granite?

b) Explain how granite is formed.

c) How can you explain the differences in the structures of granite and basalt?

d) What makes igneous rocks hard?

4 a) Name two metamorphic rocks and name the parent rocks from which each was formed.

b) Explain the ways in which metamorphic rocks can be formed.

c) How could you tell a metamorphic rock from an igneous rock?

d) Why are fossils absent from igneous rocks?

5 a) What is a sediment?

b) Explain how sediments become converted to sedimentary rocks.

c) How does the structure of sedimentary rocks indicate that the sediments from which they were formed were originally under water?

6 Make a list of the materials that have been used to build your school and the buildings near it. Classify each material under the following headings:

ii) rock (igneous, sedimentary or metamorphic)

ii) manufactured from rocks

iii) manufactured from substances other than rocks

iv) other natural substances.

9 Reactions of metals and metal compounds

Metals have many properties in common. However, they are still sufficiently different to allow them to be put to different uses.

- Tungsten has the highest melting point (3410 °C); it is used to make the filaments in light bulbs.
- Sodium has a very low melting point (98 °C) compared to tungsten; it is used as a liquid in nuclear power stations to carry the heat from the nuclear reactor to the steam turbines to generate electricity.

- Gold is a very unreactive metal; for thousands of years it has been used to make jewellery and coins.
- Mercury is the only metal that is a liquid at room temperature; it is used in thermometers.

Figure 1 ▼

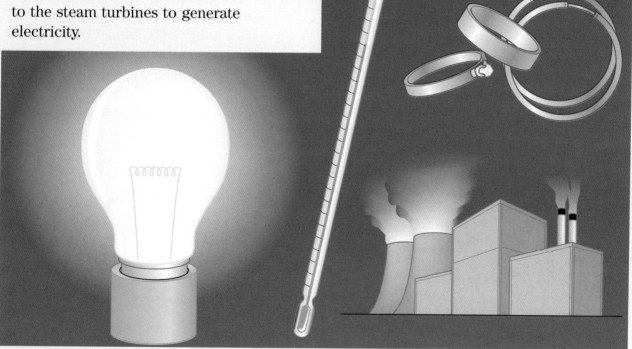

Metals

All metals have similar properties; the substances we call metals have all been grouped together because of these similar properties. Of the 92 naturally occurring elements, most are metals. Examples are aluminium, iron, copper and gold.

Most metals have the properties listed below.

- They are solids at room temperature. The exception is mercury, which is a liquid.
- Metals have a greater density than non-metals.
- Most metals have high melting points. Examples are iron 1535 °C, gold 1063 °C, copper 1083 °C, aluminium 660 °C. Exceptions are potassium 64 °C and sodium 98 °C.
- Most metals have a shiny appearance, especially when freshly cut. It is this property that makes metals useful as mirrors and as inexpensive jewellery.
- Most metals are strong. This is why they are often used to construct bridges – they are able to withstand very large forces.
- All solid metals are **malleable**; this means that metals can be hammered or bent into shape to make useful objects, such as car bodies.
- Most metals are **ductile**; this means that it is possible to pull metals into wires.
- All metals are good conductors of heat. It is this property that makes metals useful for cooking utensils and in domestic heating systems.
- All metals are very good conductors of electricity. This is why metals are used in electrical circuits.

The structure of metals

We know that metals contain atoms, but how are these atoms arranged in the metals themselves?

The way the atoms are arranged in metals must explain the properties common to all metals. Atoms are very small and we cannot see them, but we can imagine what they are like. To help us to understand the structure of metals we use a **model** (Figure 2). The atoms are represented as spheres, arranged in contact with each other. The **electrons** from the atoms are spread evenly between the nuclei of the atoms. The negative electrons attract the positive nuclei of the metal atoms and hold the metal atoms together.

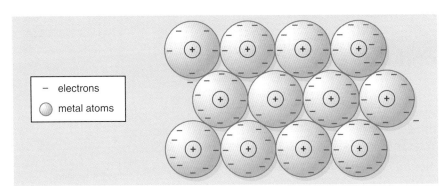

- electrons
- metal atoms

Figure 2 ◄

How good is this model?

If our model explains the properties of metals then we have a good model; if it fails then we need to devise a better model. In our model of the structure of metals we imagined the metal atoms as being in contact with each other, held together by a 'glue' of moving electrons.

We will now consider some of the properties listed above, and see how our model explains the properties.

Figure 3 ▲ The heat is conducted along the metal poker

Why are metals good conductors of heat?

If one end of a metal poker is placed in a blazing fire, after five or ten minutes the whole length of the poker will be hot. The end in the fire is heated directly by the flames. The rest of the poker receives its heat energy by conduction.

Metals are good conductors of heat because of their structure. The atoms of a metal are packed close together in a regular structure called a lattice. Between the atoms is a sea of electrons that drift through the structure. Heat from the fire causes the atoms and electrons that are heated directly to vibrate and move around more vigorously. These atoms and electrons bump into neighbouring particles, causing them to move more vigorously and passing the heat energy along the metal, see Figure 4.

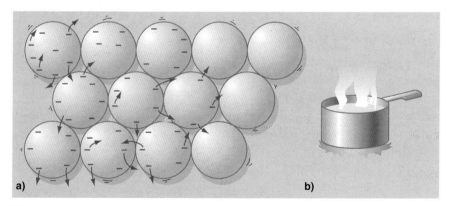

a)   b)

Figure 4 ▲

Why are metals good conductors of electricity?

An electric current is a flow of charged particles, called electrons. To conduct electricity well, metals must have electrons that can move. In metals, the electrons are free to flow easily throughout the metallic lattice structure; it is the electrons that carry the electric current, see Figure 5.

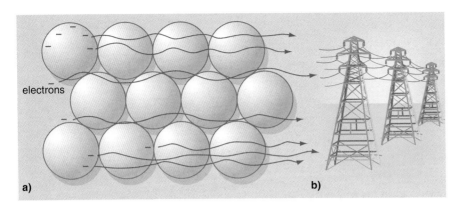

a)

b)

Figure 5 ◀

Why are metals malleable and ductile?

A metal is said to be malleable if it can be rolled or hammered
into shape. It is said to be ductile if it can be pulled into a wire.
When aluminium is bent or rolled to make foil, the atoms in it
move to new positions. To do this, the atoms have to slide over
each other while not breaking the metal. The atoms must be
touching each other and must be able to slide past each other.
The atoms in our model are able to do this, see Figure 6.

Figure 6 ▼

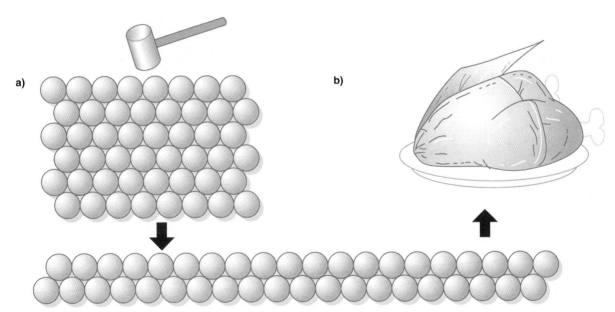

a)

b)

All of these properties of metals are explained well by the
proposed model. The model does not explain all the properties of
metal, but it explains enough of their properties to show that the
model is correct.

Non-metals

Of the 92 naturally occurring elements, the majority are metals,
the rest of them are non-metals. The properties of non-metals are
opposite to those of metals.

Non-metals:

- are poor conductors of heat and electricity (an exception is graphite, which does conduct electricity)
- tend to crumble if any attempt is made to bend or shape them
- have low melting points
- are much less dense than metals (many non-metals are gases)
- are often dull in appearance
- can be solids, liquids or gases at room temperature.

Why are non-metals poor conductors?

The main difference between metals and non-metals is that metals conduct heat and electricity well but non-metals do not. Why is this?

In order to conduct heat well, the atoms in a substance must be touching each other. In non-metals, the atoms are too far apart and there is no 'sea' of electrons, as there is in metals. The atoms or molecules are so far apart that they do not bump into each other very much, therefore the heat energy is not transferred between the atoms or molecules of a non-metal. For these reasons, non-metals are usually very poor conductors of heat.

In order to conduct electricity well, two conditions must be met. The atoms must have electrons that can move through the material and the atoms also need to be close to each other. In non-metals there are few free charge carriers, i.e. there is no sea of electrons. For this reason non-metals are not good conductors of electricity.

Non-metals use their electrons to join their atoms together to form molecules. A molecule is formed by several atoms that are joined together by sharing electrons. The electrons that would be used to carry the electric current are either held too tightly by the atoms or are used in making molecules.

Test Yourself

1   What is an element?

2   Complete these sentences. Metals are _____ conductors of electricity because they have charge carriers called _____ in them. These charge carriers have a _____ charge. In order for an electric current to flow, these charge carriers must be able to _____.

3   What is meant by the term *malleable*?

4   Explain why metals are malleable.

5   Explain why metals conduct heat well.

Luigi Galvani

An Italian called Luigi Galvani (1737–1798) was investigating the effects of electrical charges on frogs' legs. He discovered he could make the leg muscle twitch by touching it with two different metals, without a source of electricity. He decided that this was due to 'animal electricity'. Galvani's work inspired his friend Count Alessandro Volta, leading Volta to invent the electrical battery (see page 170, Chapter 12).

Figure 7 ▲

Uses of metals

Metals are very important in our everyday lives. The three most important metals to us are copper, iron and aluminium. Table 1 shows some of the uses we make of these metals.

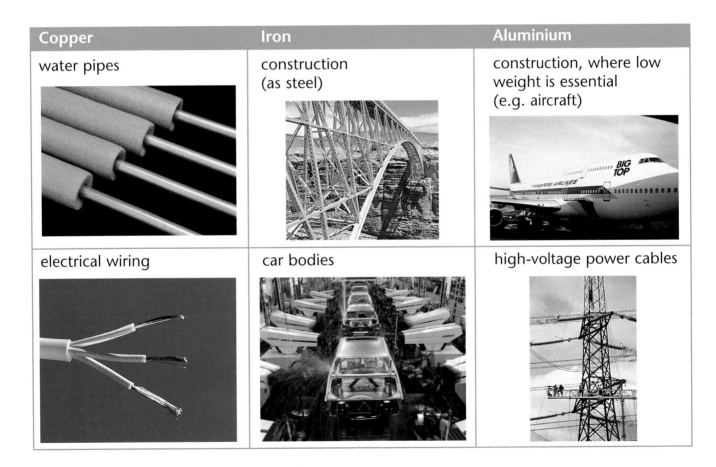

Copper	Iron	Aluminium
water pipes	construction (as steel)	construction, where low weight is essential (e.g. aircraft)
electrical wiring	car bodies	high-voltage power cables

Table 1 ▲ Some uses of copper, iron and aluminium

We also use metals, such as gold, silver and platinum, for jewellery and ornaments because they are hard-wearing and shiny.

Figure 8 ◄

Extension box

Alloys

An **alloy** is a special mixture made of two or more metals. Often an alloy is better for certain jobs than the individual metals used to make it. Alloys are made by melting one metal and adding other metals to it, to form a solution. When the solution has the correct composition it is cooled to form the solid alloy.

Solder is used to join two pieces of metal together. It is a mixture containing 63% tin and 37% lead. Solder melts at 183 °C. It is easier to use this mixture of metals for soldering than either pure tin, which melts at 232 °C, or pure lead, which melts at 327 °C.

Dentists use an alloy to fill teeth. The alloy is made of silver, tin, copper, zinc and mercury. Alloys containing mercury are called 'amalgams'. When first mixed together, dental amalgam is soft enough for the dentist to push it into a cavity in a tooth, but it soon becomes much harder. Dental amalgam fillings are cheap and last a long time. Recently there have been concerns that the mercury in fillings made from dental amalgam might be harmful. So far there is no evidence to suggest that it is.

Sometimes a small amount of a non-metal is also added to an alloy. The most important non-metal for this is carbon. Carbon is added to iron to make it into steel. Steel is an important material, used to make many things from engines to kitchen knives. The 'stainless steel' used to make kitchen knives, among many other things, has chromium added to it to stop it rusting.

Extension box

Bronze, an alloy of copper and tin, has been used to make weapons for thousands of years – the tin makes the bronze much harder than pure copper.

There are also some very modern uses for alloys, for example in keyhole surgery (where a surgeon performs the operation through a small hole in the body, to speed up healing and reduce scarring). At body temperature these medical alloys are flexible, but they harden if they are heated. At the end of an operation, the surgeon's incisions must be closed up. This is usually done with a needle and special thread. However, there is not enough room to do this in keyhole surgery. Instead, a small loop of the flexible alloy is fitted through the tissues to be joined. The alloy is then heated by passing an electric current through it. The two points close together, holding the tissue in place.

Figure 9 ▼

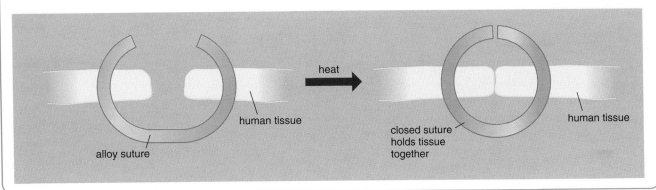

Reactions of metals

Reactions of metals with acids

If a piece of zinc metal is placed into a test tube of hydrochloric acid, the metal dissolves and a gas is given off. The zinc dissolves to form a solution of a salt, zinc chloride, and the gas given off is hydrogen.

$$\text{zinc} + \text{hydrochloric acid} \rightarrow \text{zinc chloride} + \text{hydrogen}$$
$$\text{Zn} + 2\text{HCl} \rightarrow \text{ZnCl}_2 + \text{H}_2$$

If the solution remaining at the end of the reaction is evaporated, crystals of zinc chloride are formed.

Metals that react with acids always give a salt and hydrogen. The general reaction can be represented by a word equation:

$$\text{metal} + \text{acid} \rightarrow \text{metal salt} + \text{hydrogen gas}$$

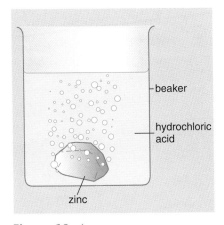

Figure 10 ▲

The salt formed depends on *both* the metal and the acid used, as shown in Table 2.

Metal	Hydrochloric acid	Sulphuric acid	Nitric acid
zinc	zinc chloride	zinc sulphate	zinc nitrate
iron	iron chloride	iron sulphate	iron nitrate
magnesium	magnesium chloride	magnesium sulphate	magnesium nitrate

Table 2 ▲

You can test for hydrogen gas by lighting a test tube of the gas, which burns with a squeaky pop.

If copper or silver is added to hydrochloric acid it does not dissolve and no hydrogen is formed. Copper and silver are not reactive enough to react with acids.

Reactions of metal carbonates with acids

Many rocks contain metal carbonates. Geologists often carry a small bottle of acid with them to test for rocks that contain carbonates. Metal carbonates react with acids to give carbon dioxide; the fizzing produced allows carbonate rocks to be identified easily.

The general word equation for the reaction between metal carbonates and an acid is:

metal carbonate + acid → metal salt + carbon dioxide + water

Here are some word equations and symbol equations for the reactions of three metal carbonates with sulphuric acid, nitric acid or hydrochloric acid. If you need to remind yourself about symbol equations, then look at page 77, Chapter 6.

copper carbonate + sulphuric acid → copper sulphate + carbon dioxide + water

$$CuCO_3 + H_2SO_4 \rightarrow CuSO_4 + CO_2 + H_2O$$

zinc carbonate + nitric acid → zinc nitrate + carbon dioxide + water

$$ZnCO_3 + 2HNO_3 \rightarrow Zn(NO_3)_2 + CO_2 + H_2O$$

magnesium carbonate + hydrochloric acid → magnesium chloride + carbon dioxide + water

$$MgCO_3 + 2HCl \rightarrow MgCl_2 + CO_2 + H_2O$$

Test Yourself

6   Write a word equation for the reaction between:
  a) calcium and sulphuric acid
  b) calcium and hydrochloric acid.

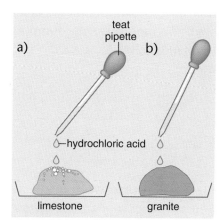

Figure 11 ▲   a) Limestone is nearly pure calcium carbonate, so there is fizzing. b) Granite is not a carbonate, so there is no fizzing

In each case, you can find lots of evidence that a reaction has taken place:

- the solid carbonate dissolves
- bubbles of carbon dioxide gas are formed
- energy is released (see below).

The test for carbon dioxide gas is that, if it is bubbled through limewater, it will cause the limewater to go cloudy. A reaction has occurred between the carbon dioxide and the limewater. The equation for this reaction is the following:

calcium   + carbon   → calcium   + water
hydroxide   dioxide   carbonate
(limewater)

$$Ca(OH)_2 + CO_2 \rightarrow CaCO_3 + H_2O$$

It is the formation of calcium carbonate that causes the limewater to go cloudy.

The reaction between calcium carbonate and acid is very useful. Acids are used to remove limescale (calcium carbonate) from kettles. The limescale needs to be removed as it reduces the efficiency of the heating element and wastes energy.

In the case of copper carbonate reacting with an acid, there is further evidence of reaction. Copper carbonate is pale green; the solution that forms is blue as it contains a copper salt in solution.

If a metal carbonate is added to an acid and the reaction mixture is stirred with a thermometer, we may see further evidence of reaction. The temperature increases during the reaction, so heat energy must be given out as the metal carbonate reacts. Heat changes, detectable by a change in temperature, are evidence for a chemical reaction.

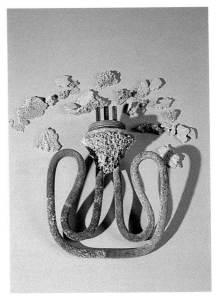

Figure 12 ▲   Limescale has coated this kettle element

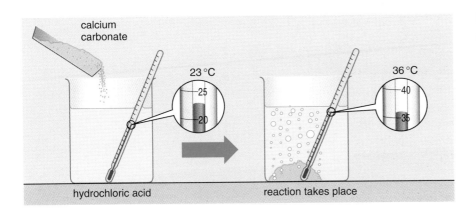

Figure 13 ◄   When reactions occur the temperature changes

Reactions of metal oxides with acids

You may remember from Chapter 3 (page 30) that sulphuric acid is used to remove rust from iron before the iron is painted. Rust is iron oxide and the sulphuric acid dissolves it, forming a salt and water. The dissolving of the rust is evidence of a chemical reaction.

$$\text{iron oxide} + \text{sulphuric acid} \rightarrow \text{iron sulphate} + \text{water}$$
$$Fe_2O_3 + 3H_2SO_4 \rightarrow Fe_2(SO_4)_3 + 3H_2O$$

All metal oxides react with acids, to form a salt and water. The general word equation is:

$$\text{metal oxide} + \text{acid} \rightarrow \text{metal salt} + \text{water}$$

Since there is no gas produced, no bubbles are formed during the reaction.

Extension box

A salt is formed whenever an acid reacts with a metal, a metal carbonate or a metal oxide.

Solutions of all acids contain positive hydrogen ions (H^+) and an ion with a negative charge. The negative ion in an acid depends on what the acid is (Table 3).

Acid	Formula of acid	Negative ion	Formula of ion
hydrochloric acid	HCl	chloride	Cl^-
nitric acid	HNO_3	nitrate	NO_3^-
sulphuric acid	H_2SO_4	sulphate	SO_4^{2-}

Table 3 ▲

A salt results when the hydrogen ions in an acid are replaced by metal ions (Table 4).

Acid	Formula of acid	Replace hydrogen with	Salt	Formula of salt
hydrochloric acid	HCl	sodium ions, Na^+	sodium chloride	NaCl
nitric acid	HNO_3	zinc ions, Zn^{2+}	zinc nitrate	$Zn(NO_3)_2$
sulphuric acid	H_2SO_4	copper ions, Cu^{2+}	copper sulphate	$CuSO_4$

Table 4 ▲

Extension box continued

Notice that in the salts the positive and negative charges balance exactly – this requirement decides the formula of the salt.

- In hydrochloric acid, the one H^+ is replaced by one Na^+, so sodium chloride has the formula NaCl.
- In making zinc nitrate the hydrogen ion has to be replaced by a zinc ion. The zinc ion has two positive charges, so two nitrate ions with one negative charge each are needed to balance the charges. Zinc nitrate therefore has the formula $Zn(NO_3)_2$. Notice that the NO_3 in the formula has a bracket round it, then a subscript '2', to show that two complete NO_3^- ions are needed.
- When copper sulphate is formed, two hydrogen ions, each with one positive charge, are replaced by a copper ion with two positive charges. Copper sulphate therefore has the formula $CuSO_4$.

Test Yourself

7   Use the table of positive and negative ions below to write down the chemical formula of the following salts.

Positive ion	Symbol	Negative ion	Symbol
lithium	Li^+	chloride	Cl^-
sodium	Na^+	nitrate	NO_3^-
potassium	K^+	sulphate	SO_4^{2-}
magnesium	Mg^{2+}		
copper	Cu^{2+}		
aluminium	Al^{3+}		

a) sodium hydroxide
b) potassium chloride
c) magnesium sulphate
d) copper nitrate
e) aluminium chloride
f) lithium sulphate
g) aluminium nitrate
h) aluminium sulphate.

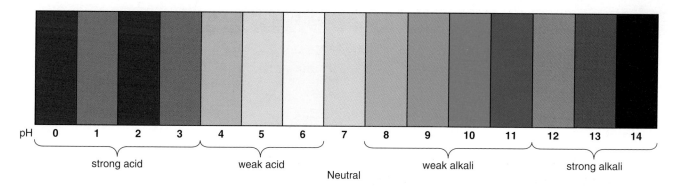

Figure 14 ▲ The colours of Universal Indicator at various pH values

Acids and alkalis

The pH scale is used to measure how acid or alkaline a substance is (see page 32, Chapter 3).

When an acid and an alkali are mixed to give a solution of pH 7, **neutralisation** has taken place. It should be possible to mix exactly the right amount of an acid with an alkali to give a solution that has a pH of 7. However, we are unlikely to be able to mix the acid and alkali in exactly the right amounts by chance.

A better way to tackle the problem might be the following:

- take some acid and determine its pH with universal indicator
- then add 10 drops of alkali from a dropping pipette
- determine the pH of the solution again
- stop adding alkali when the pH reaches 7.

The drawback with this method is that the solution might become neutral after an amount of alkali equal to 32 drops had been added. Since we are adding the alkali in 10 drop quantities, we will still need to add more alkali after 30 drops have been added, but will have added too much alkali when we have added 40 drops. The final solution would not have a pH of 7, but a pH of more than 7.

Test Yourself

8   Think of ways to improve the method outlined above.

Neutralisation

When acids and alkalis react, the products are always a salt and water:

$$acid + alkali \rightarrow salt + water$$

You need to be able to recall the names of the following common acids and alkalis.

Acids	Alkalis
hydrochloric acid	sodium hydroxide
sulphuric acid	potassium hydroxide
nitric acid	calcium hydroxide

Table 5 ▲

Remember that acids and alkalis are can be harmful, corrosive or irritant, depending on how concentrated they are. You should always wear eye protection and rinse away any spills or splashes with plenty of water.

Be careful not to confuse the terms 'salt' and 'a salt'. 'Salt' is the everyday name for sodium chloride. 'A salt' is any substance, including sodium chloride, which has been made by a neutralisation reaction between an acid and an alkali.

Making salts

To make a salt by neutralisation, we need an accurate way of adding the alkali to the acid. We also need a way of testing the pH of the solution, so we know when neutralisation has occurred.

We can use indicators to tell whether a solution is acidic or alkaline – the indicator changes colour as the pH changes. You have seen this list of indicators before, in Chapter 3 (page 32).

Indicator	Colour in acid	Colour in alkali
litmus	red	blue
phenolphthalein	colourless	pink
methyl orange	red	yellow

Table 6 ▲

A better way of finding out exactly how much acid and alkali must be mixed to give a neutral solution is to use a technique known as **titration**.

To carry out a titration you need the following apparatus:

- measuring cylinder
- burette
- conical flask.

The measuring cylinder is used to measure a certain volume of liquid, usually $25 \, cm^3$. The burette can hold $50 \, cm^3$ of liquid and has graduations every $1.0 \, cm^3$, each of which is further divided into $0.10 \, cm^3$ divisions. By careful use of the tap, any volume of liquid can be a measured out, to an accuracy of $0.1 \, cm^3$.

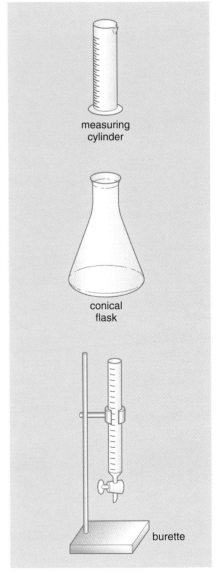

Figure 15 ▲ Apparatus used for titration experiments

measuring cylinder

conical flask

burette

One liquid is placed in the conical flask and the other is added to the conical flask from the burette. The two liquids are then mixed in the conical flask. A conical flask is used, rather than a beaker, because the contents can be swirled to mix the acid and alkali without them spilling so easily.

To carry out a titration, the following steps need to be followed.

1 Measure out 25 cm³ of acid using a measuring cylinder.
2 Add the acid to a 250 cm³ conical flask.
3 Add 3 or 4 drops of phenolphthalein indicator. Phenolphthalein is colourless in acid, pink in alkali.
4 Fill the burette with alkali to the zero mark. Note that the surface of the alkali in the burette is curved into a meniscus – you read the measurement at the bottom of this meniscus.
5 Open the burette tap to allow the alkali to run into the acid. You will see that the indicator turns pink around the added alkali, but this disappears when the contents of the conical flask are swirled.
6 Keep adding alkali, adding it more slowly as the pink alkaline colour of the indicator lasts longer.
7 Finally, add the alkali drop by drop to the solution stopping as soon as it just turns a permanent pink colour.
8 Read the final volume shown on the burette.

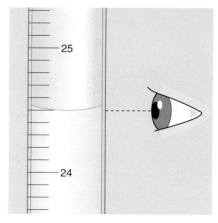

Figure 16 ▲ The correct reading on the burette is 24.50 cm³

Exactly the right amount of alkali has now been added to neutralise the acid. In the flask we have a solution of the salt, but we also have the indicator.

To make crystals of the salt free of indicator, the whole experiment has to be repeated without step 3 – i.e. without the indicator. We know how much acid and alkali were used in the first experiment. As a result, we can measure 25 cm³ of the acid into a beaker using the measuring cylinder and then add exactly the same volume of alkali from the burette as was used in the first experiment. The solution is neutral, but contains no indicator to colour the salt. The solution can now be evaporated to about one-third of its volume and left to cool, when crystals of the salt will form.

The metal contained in a salt depends on the alkali used:

- to prepare sodium salts, use sodium hydroxide
- to prepare potassium salts, use potassium hydroxide
- to prepare calcium salts, use calcium hydroxide.

The other part of the salt, the non-metal part, depends on the acid used:

- to prepare chlorides, use hydrochloric acid
- to prepare sulphates, use sulphuric acid
- to prepare nitrates, use nitric acid.

Figure 17 ▲ Carrying out a titration

Uses of salts

Table 7 gives the names of some salts and their uses.

Name of salt	Uses
sodium chloride	• in the food industry as a flavouring and as a preservative • mixed with grit to remove ice from roads
potassium sulphate	• to make fertilisers
sodium carbonate	• to make glass
sodium hydrogencarbonate	• in baking powder
calcium carbonate	• to make cement, glass and iron
calcium sulphate	• to make building plaster or plaster of Paris

Table 7 ▲ Some salts and their uses

Test Yourself

9 Name the acid and alkali needed to make each of the following salts:
a) sodium nitrate
b) calcium chloride
c) potassium sulphate.

10 What property of metals is most important when they are used to make the following things?
a) the reflector in a car headlight
b) a weight belt for a skin diver
c) a pan support on a gas cooker
d) a string for a guitar
e) a helicopter
f) a frying pan.

Summary

When you have finished studying this chapter, you should understand that:

✔ All metals have similar properties.

✔ The atoms in a metal are packed closely together in a lattice structure with a 'sea' of free electrons, which move in between the atoms.

✔ The properties of metals are a consequence of this structure.

✔ Non-metals have properties that are usually the opposite of those of metals.

✔ Metals have important uses in everyday life.

✔ Most metals react with acids to give a salt and hydrogen.

✔ Metal carbonates react with acids to give carbon dioxide, a salt and water.

✔ Metal oxides react with acids to give a salt and water.

✔ Chemical reactions produce new materials.

✔ Energy changes provide evidence of a chemical reaction.

✔ Acids and alkalis neutralise each other to give a salt and water.

✔ Acids and alkalis need to be handled carefully.

End-of-Chapter Questions

1 Explain in your own words the following key terms you have met in this chapter:

malleable

ductile

model

electron

alloy

neutralisation

titration

burette

2 Here are some instructions for making copper sulphate from sulphuric acid and copper carbonate, but the instructions are in the wrong order.

A Add some copper carbonate until excess copper carbonate is present.

B Warm the acid.

C Add some sulphuric acid to a beaker.

D Filter off the excess copper carbonate.

E Leave to cool.

F Evaporate the solution to about half its volume.

G Filter off the crystals and dry them.

a) Put the steps in the correct order.

b) Give two reasons why excess copper carbonate was added to the acid.

c) How could you tell that all the acid had reacted?

d) What was the purpose of warming the acid?

e) Explain, in terms of particles, why crystals form when the solution is allowed to cool.

End-of-Chapter Questions continued

3 Alan was given three mixtures to identify by his teacher. He added acid to each of the mixtures in turn and tested for any gases given off. His results are shown in the table.

The mixtures are:

i) a mixture of a magnesium oxide and copper

ii) copper oxide and sodium carbonate

iii) magnesium and zinc oxide.

Mixture	Observation when hydrochloric acid was added
A	Gas given off which turned limewater milky. Mixture dissolved to give a blue solution.
B	Gas given off which burned with a squeaky pop. Mixture dissolved to give a colourless solution.
C	No gas given off. Some of the mixture did not dissolve.

a) Explain, giving reasons for your choice, which mixture could be which.

b) Write word equations and symbol equations for the reactions that took place.

10 Patterns of reactivity

Gold was used by humans long before iron was. This is not because there is more gold in the Earth, but because gold is so unreactive. Gold does not combine with other elements and is found in the ground as the pure metal. Some metals are very reactive and are never found in their pure form. Nowadays we purify metals using electricity, in a process called electrolysis. The most important of the metals obtained using electricity is aluminium, which was first made in large quantities in 1886. When aluminium was first purified it was very expensive – in 1880 it cost £220 000 per tonne. The wealthy impressed their dinner guests by having their cutlery and plates made of it. Emperor Napoleon III's best cutlery was made from aluminium, with a gold set as second best! By 1910, the cost had fallen to £85 per tonne and we now use aluminium for disposable drinks cans.

Figure 1 ▶ Napoleon's aluminium tableware

Discovering metals

- There are about a hundred elements known – most of them are metals.
- We use metals a lot in our everyday lives.
- Some metals react quite quickly with air and water, but others seem unaffected.

A fairly good guide to the reactivity of a metal is its date of discovery. The least reactive metals were discovered first; for thousands of years gold, silver, copper, iron and lead were the only metals known.

Date of discovery	Examples of metals discovered		
known for thousands of years	gold, silver, copper, iron, lead		
1700–1800	cobalt, zinc, nickel, titanium		
1800–1900	sodium, magnesium, aluminium		

Table 1 ▲

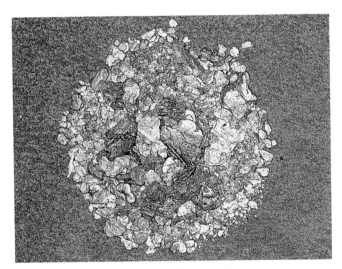

Figure 2 ▲   Gold panned from a river

Metals, such as gold and silver, can be dug out of the ground as pure substances. This is why they were discovered first. Gold and silver can be left in contact with air and water for thousands of years without reacting. We can conclude that gold and silver are very unreactive.

Reactive metals combine with oxygen in the air or with water and are only found naturally as compounds. As an example of these differences in reactivity, archaeologists sometimes find a sword with a very rusty iron blade, but with the gold handle looking like new.

Uses of metals and their reactivity

For thousands of years gold has been used for making things that had to last a long time, such as coins and jewellery. This ability to last has made gold very valuable – it is still used for jewellery today, but has become too costly for coins. Metals, such as copper, or the alloy bronze (made of copper and tin) were used to make statues and weapons because they lasted better than iron articles. Even thousands of years ago it was realised that some metals were less reactive than others.

Test Yourself

1   Pick a metallic element discovered between 1700 and 1900. Try to find out exactly when the metal was discovered and what it can be used for. You may like to look at the website http://www.chemicalelements.com/

Science Scope: CHEMISTRY

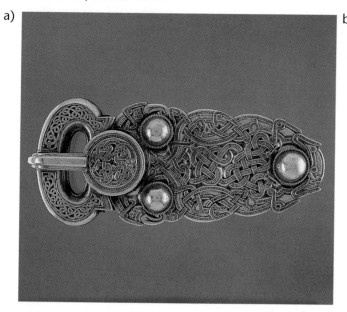 

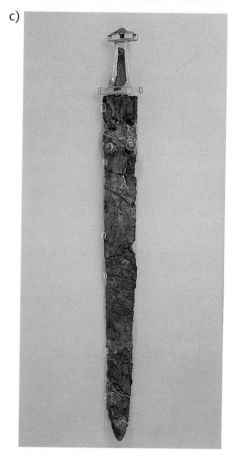

Figure 3 ▲ a) A gold belt buckle, b) bronze hanging bowl, the copper in the bronze has turned green, and c) an iron sword that has rusted. All of these were found in the burial mound of an Anglo-Saxon king in East Anglia, dating from the 7th century AD

Look at the items in Figure 3. Notice that the gold buckle looks like new; that the bronze bowl is covered with some green corrosion because it contains copper; but that the iron sword is badly rusted. By comparing how these three metals corrode, we can arrange them in an order of increasing reactivity:

- gold (least reactive)
- copper
- iron (most reactive).

Finding the reactivity of metals

There is a big difference in the reactivity of iron and gold that is easy to see. When we start to consider other metals, we find that many do not differ much in their reactivity. We need to find some other ways of working out just how reactive metals are. We will find out how this is done with the following nine metals, listed here in alphabetical order:

- aluminium
- calcium
- copper
- gold
- iron
- magnesium
- potassium
- sodium
- zinc.

130

It is possible to construct a **reactivity series** by comparing how easily different metals react. A reactivity series is a list of metals from the most reactive to the least reactive. The reactivity series is based on experiments designed to find out how easily metals react with:

- oxygen in the air
- water
- acids
- aqueous solutions of salts of another metal.

All the known metals *could* be included in a reactivity series, but the nine metals listed above are enough to show how the reactivity series works.

Figure 4 ▲

Reactions of metals with oxygen

All these nine metals, except copper and gold, react with oxygen in the air. Some of the metals need to be in the form of a powder or a fine wire before they burn in air. For example, steel wool burns easily and sparklers contain iron powder – the sparks are small particles of iron burning in the air. Old-fashioned flash bulbs, the sort you see newspaper photographers in black and white films using, contained magnesium foil or wire.

The reaction with oxygen can be used to tell the difference between very reactive and unreactive metals, which are far apart in the reactivity series. It is not a very good way of telling apart metals that are closer together in the reactivity series.

a)

b)

c)

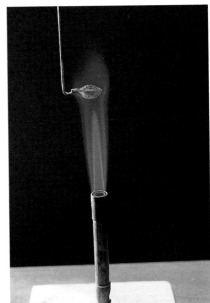

Figure 5 ▲ a) Sodium, b) magnesium and c) iron burning in oxygen

Test Yourself

2 Part of the reactivity series is:

sodium
magnesium   reactivity decreases
iron
copper

Which metal would you expect to burn best in oxygen and which worst?

3 The photographs in Figure 6 show sodium, magnesium and iron burning in oxygen. Do they burn as you would expect from their places in the reactivity series shown in Question 2?

4 Write a word equation for the reaction when iron burns in oxygen.

5 Chlorine is also a reactive gas. The pictures below show sodium and iron burning in chlorine. Work out which metal is which.

6 When metals burn in oxygen they form oxides. For example:

sodium + oxygen → sodium oxide
$4Na$ $+ O_2$ $→ 2Na_2O$

When metals burn in chlorine they form chlorides. Write a word equation and a symbol equation for the reaction when sodium burns in chlorine.

Reactions of metals with water

The reactions of our nine metals with water show up the differences in reactivity better than burning them in air. Table 2 shows the results, again listed in alphabetical order.

Metal	Description of its reaction with water	Products of the reaction
aluminium	no reaction with cold water. Can react with steam, but the aluminium must be heated strongly	hydrogen + aluminium oxide
calcium	brisk – a steady stream of hydrogen bubbles is given off	hydrogen + calcium hydroxide
copper	no reaction	–
gold	no reaction	–
iron	no reaction with cold water. Can react with steam, but the iron must be red hot	hydrogen + iron oxide
magnesium	no reaction with cold water. A reaction occurs if the magnesium is heated in steam	hydrogen + magnesium oxide
potassium	violent – the metal melts and the hydrogen formed catches fire	hydrogen + potassium hydroxide
sodium	vigorous – the metal melts, but the hydrogen formed does not catch fire	hydrogen + sodium hydroxide
zinc	no reaction with cold water. Can react with steam, but the zinc must be heated strongly	hydrogen + zinc oxide

Table 2 ▲

These reactions can be summarised by word equations and the corresponding symbol equations.

a)

$$\text{sodium} + \text{water} \rightarrow \text{sodium hydroxide} + \text{hydrogen}$$
$$2Na + 2H_2O \rightarrow 2NaOH + H_2$$

$$\text{magnesium} + \text{water} \rightarrow \text{magnesium oxide} + \text{hydrogen}$$
$$2Mg + H_2O \rightarrow 2MgO + H_2$$

Sodium and potassium are so reactive that they are stored under oil to prevent air and water reaching them.

The results in Table 2 can be used to list the nine metals in a reactivity series. Just using the results from Table 2, we cannot distinguish between aluminium and zinc and between copper and gold. However, if you look back at Figure 3, you can see that copper is more reactive than gold. The order is:

potassium
sodium
calcium
magnesium
aluminium/zinc | decreasing reactivity
iron
copper
gold

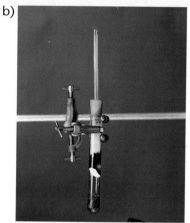

b)

Figure 6 ▲   a) Potassium reacting with cold water; b) magnesium reacting with steam

Test Yourself

7   a) Use the colour chart for universal indicator to work out the pH of the solution formed when sodium and water react.
    b) Is the solution acidic or alkaline?
    c) What colour would the indicator be if the solution had been neutral?

Reactions of metals with acids

The reactivity series found with the reactions of metals with water is the same when acids are used. However, the reactions of potassium and sodium are so violent that they are too dangerous to carry out in a school laboratory.

Hydrogen is always one product of any reaction between a metal and an acid. If sulphuric acid (H_2SO_4) is used, the sulphate of the metal is formed. If hydrochloric acid (HCl) is used, the chloride of the metal is formed.

Metal	Description of its reaction with acid	Products of the reaction with sulphuric acid	Products of the reaction with hydrochloric acid
potassium sodium			
calcium magnesium aluminium zinc iron	metal dissolves and hydrogen is given off. The reaction is slower as the list is descended	hydrogen + a solution of the metal sulphate	hydrogen + a solution of the metal chloride
copper gold	no reaction		

Table 3 ▲

Here are the word equations with the corresponding symbol equations for the reaction of metals with acids:

calcium + hydrochloric acid → calcium chloride + hydrogen
Ca + 2HCl → $CaCl_2$ + H_2

zinc + sulphuric acid → zinc sulphate + hydrogen
Zn + H_2SO_4 → $ZnSO_4$ + H_2

On the basis of their reactions so far, our nine metals can be listed in order of decreasing reactivity. We can decide that aluminium is more reactive than zinc by using displacement reactions – which are discussed later (see page 136). You should try to learn both the names and symbols of these metals.

potassium, K
sodium, Na
calcium, Ca
magnesium, Mg
aluminium, Al — decreasing reactivity
zinc, Zn
iron, Fe
copper, Cu
gold, Au

Test Yourself

8 Why are sodium and potassium not reacted with acids to find out where they come in the reactivity series?

The unusual behaviour of aluminium

Aluminium is much more reactive than iron but it seems to corrode less in air. Why is this?

Aluminium reacts readily with air, but a thin layer of aluminium oxide forms on the surface and protects the metal underneath from any further reaction. Aluminium seems to be less reactive than it actually is, unless the oxide layer is scraped off before carrying out any reactions.

The thermit reaction

The thermit reaction shows that aluminium is more reactive than iron. In the thermit reaction, aluminium is used to remove the oxygen from iron oxide. This is a displacement reaction, but it differs from the displacement reactions discussed above in that it occurs between two solids.

A mixture of aluminium powder and iron oxide is ignited using a piece of magnesium ribbon as a fuse. There is a violent reaction, during which aluminium oxide and iron are formed. The reaction is so violent that the temperature of the mixture rises to above the melting point of iron, about 1500 °C. The thermit reaction is used to mend railway lines, by allowing the molten iron to run onto the ends of the broken rails.

iron oxide + aluminium → iron + aluminium oxide

$$Fe_2O_3 + 2Al \rightarrow 2Fe + Al_2O_3$$

Figure 7 ▲ The thermit reaction being used to mend railway lines

Displacement reactions

When a metal is added to a solution of a salt of another metal, a reaction is sometimes seen. Reactions of this type are known as **displacement reactions**. Whether a reaction occurs, or not, depends on the relative positions of the two metals in the reactivity series. The flow diagram in Figure 8 will help you to work out which of two metals is the more reactive.

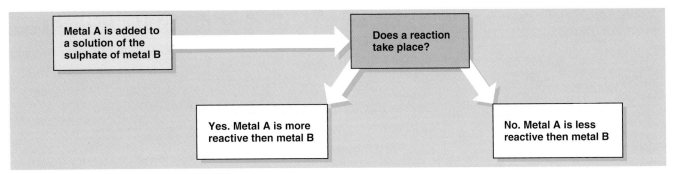

Look at Figure 8. Zinc is added to a solution of copper sulphate. The zinc gradually dissolves in the copper sulphate a) and a pink deposit of copper metal forms at the bottom of the beaker b). The solution gradually loses its blue colour c) as the zinc reacts with the copper sulphate. Zinc, the more reactive metal, has displaced copper ions from solution, see Figure 9.

Figure 8 ▲

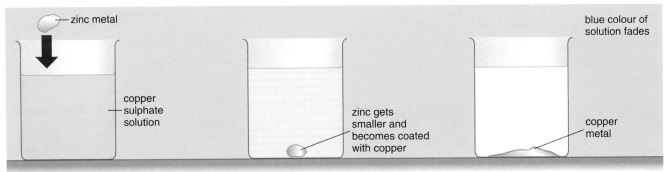

Figure 9 ▲

In some reactions, only a dark coating appears on the more reactive metal. However, this is enough to show that a reaction has taken place.

A reactivity series using displacement reactions can be obtained by:

- cleaning small samples of each metal
- adding each metal to aqueous solutions of the salts of the other metals
- looking to see whether a reaction occurs.

The results for magnesium, aluminium, zinc, iron and copper are summarised in Table 4. The metals potassium, sodium and calcium are too reactive to use with aqueous solutions.

Table 4 ▼

✔ = reaction observed
✗ = no reaction observed

	Magnesium sulphate solution	Aluminium sulphate solution	Zinc sulphate solution	Iron sulphate solution	Copper sulphate solution
magnesium		✔	✔	✔	✔
aluminium	✗		✔	✔	✔
zinc	✗	✗		✔	✔
iron	✗	✗	✗		✔
copper	✗	✗	✗	✗	

Sample word equations and the corresponding symbol equations are shown here:

$$\text{magnesium} + \text{zinc sulphate} \rightarrow \text{magnesium sulphate} + \text{zinc}$$
$$Mg + ZnSO_4 \rightarrow MgSO_4 + Zn$$

$$\text{iron} + \text{copper sulphate} \rightarrow \text{iron sulphate} + \text{copper}$$
$$Fe + CuSO_4 \rightarrow FeSO_4 + Cu$$

The extraction of gold

Gold has been known and used for thousands of years. It is a very unreactive metal and because of this it occurs naturally as pure gold. Most other metals (iron, copper, zinc, etc.) are found combined with other elements as chemical compounds.

In the gold rush of the mid 1850s, nuggets of gold were found in streams by 'panning'. Panning involved swirling a mixture of sand, grit and small particles of gold in a shallow pan. The heavier gold particles remained in the pan but the sand and grit got washed out. Fairly soon the large nuggets and gold deposits in streams were used up. Any gold remaining had to be extracted from the solid rock, in which it was found only in very small amounts.

Figure 10 ▼ Gold prospectors, Dakota USA 1857

Test Yourself

9 Nickel comes between iron and copper in the reactivity series. Nickel sulphate is a green solution.
   a) What would you expect to happen when copper is added to a solution of nickel sulphate?
   b) What would you expect to happen when iron is added to a solution of nickel sulphate?
   c) From its place in the reactivity series, suggest a use for nickel.

Ideas and Evidence   Gold production

The Swedish chemist Karl Scheele (1742–1786) discovered that gold would dissolve in solutions of sodium cyanide. (This discovery allowed articles to be gold plated.)

The Scottish chemist John MacArthur realised that it should be possible to extract gold from rock by dissolving the gold with cyanide. He also discovered that the gold dissolved far more quickly if air was blown through the cyanide solution. In 1887 he was granted a patent for his process.

MacArthur crushed up the rock containing gold and put it into a solution of sodium cyanide through which air was blown. The gold reacts with the cyanide solution and dissolves. The crushed rock was filtered off from the solution containing the gold. Powdered zinc was then added to the solution and the zinc displaced the gold. Any remaining zinc was simply dissolved away with acid, which did not affect the gold. The process was a commercial success and the production of gold doubled in the next 20 years. However, it wasn't until the 1950s that the chemistry of the process was fully understood.

Extension box

The position of hydrogen in the reactivity series

Figure 11 shows the reactions of a range of metals with an acid. You can see from the photographs that copper doesn't give hydrogen with acid. The other metals, including iron, do give hydrogen. The more rapid the reaction the higher the metal is in the reactivity series.

If we include hydrogen in our reactivity series, it comes between iron and copper:

potassium, K
sodium, Na
calcium, Ca
magnesium, Mg
aluminium, Al
zinc, Zn
iron, Fe
hydrogen, H
copper, Cu
gold, Au

decreasing reactivity

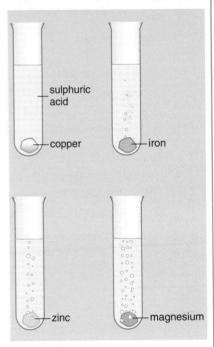

Figure 11 ▲

Metals such as copper and gold are below hydrogen in the reactivity series and never give hydrogen when placed in water or acids. It is useful to have hydrogen in the reactivity series, because it gives us an idea of which metals can be used for making things that have to be in contact with water or acids without reacting.

Extension box

Electricity and the reactivity series

Figure 12 shows how electricity can be made using copper and zinc and a beaker of acid. Any two different metals will work, but the further apart the metals are in the reactivity series the bigger voltage you get.

The electrons move from the more reactive metal, through the wire, to the less reactive metal. Reactive metals give up their electrons more easily.

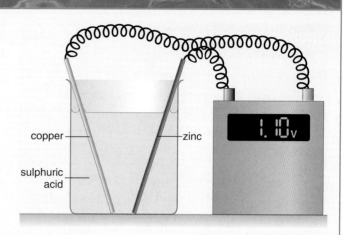

Figure 12 ▲

Test Yourself

10

magnesium
aluminium
zinc
iron
copper
gold

decreasing reactivity

a) Which two metals in this reactivity series would give the biggest voltage if used in a battery?

b) Choose two metals which are likely to give only a small voltage.

11 Sacha made three batteries, each using copper and another metal chosen from iron, magnesium and zinc. The voltages she got are in the table.

a) Complete the table to show the other metal used.

Cell	Voltage	Other metal used
A	1.1 V	
B	2.7 V	
C	0.8 V	

b) What voltage would you predict if Sacha made a battery from copper and a metal between iron and zinc in the reactivity series?

What use is the reactivity series?

The reactivity series helps us to choose the right metal for the right job.

- Unreactive metals, such as gold and silver, are used to make things that we want to last for a long time.
- Copper is good for making water pipes because it does not react with water, even if left in contact with it for a long time.
- Iron is strong and cheap, so it is the most important metal for making things in everyday life, such as cars, bridges, railway lines and hundreds of other things. The rusting of iron is a nuisance, but iron is so cheap and useful that we can cope with this problem by protecting the iron, for example by painting it.

The reactivity series helps us to invent an even better way of protecting iron – **galvanising**. The iron object is coated with zinc. Because zinc is more reactive than iron, the zinc corrodes first, leaving the iron free of rust.

a)

b)

Figure 13 ▲ a) galvanised dustbins and b) a rusty steel girder that was not galvanised

The extraction of metals

Most metals are found in the Earth as compounds, usually oxides. To obtain the metal the oxygen must be removed from the oxide. How this is done depends on the position of the metal in the reactivity series.

Extraction of iron and zinc

Iron is found near the lower end of the reactivity series. Iron and other metals in this part of the series, such as zinc, can be extracted by smelting with carbon.

Smelting involves heating the oxide of the metal with carbon in a furnace. The carbon removes the oxygen from the metal, forming carbon dioxide.

$$\text{metal oxide} + \text{carbon} \xrightarrow{\text{heat}} \text{metal} + \text{carbon dioxide}$$

For example:

$$\text{iron oxide} + \text{carbon} \xrightarrow{\text{heat}} \text{iron} + \text{carbon dioxide}$$

$$2Fe_2O_3 + 3C \rightarrow 4Fe + 3CO_2$$

Extraction of reactive metals

Reactive metals such as magnesium and sodium are too reactive to be extracted by heating with carbon. They have to be extracted by electrolysis.

Electrolysis involves passing an electric current through a molten compound of the metal, usually its chloride. The positive metal ions in the compound are converted to the metal by gaining electrons from the power supply.

$$\text{positive metal ions} + \text{electrons} \rightarrow \text{metal atoms}$$

$$Na^+ + e^- \rightarrow Na$$

The reactivity series also helps us to make other very reactive metals, such as titanium. Titanium is a very important metal – like aluminium it is light and does not corrode. Titanium has to be made by reacting a titanium compound with sodium or magnesium in a displacement reaction. The idea of making titanium this way came from knowing about the reactivity series.

Extension box

Why are some metals more reactive than others?

The atoms of all elements have electrons orbiting round the nucleus. The electrons are held in their orbits by the attraction of the positive protons in the nucleus. When metals react, their atoms lose one or more electrons. This leaves the atom with an overall positive charge: it has become what chemists call a positive ion.

- Some metals, such as potassium, lose their electrons very easily and are reactive.
- Metals such as copper lose their electrons only with difficulty and are much less reactive.

We have seen that potassium is more reactive than sodium. This is because the bigger potassium atom finds it easier to lose electrons than the smaller sodium atom. Protons and electrons attract each other in all atoms because of their opposite electrical charges. However, the protons and electrons are further apart in potassium, so the attraction is less and the electrons can be lost more easily.

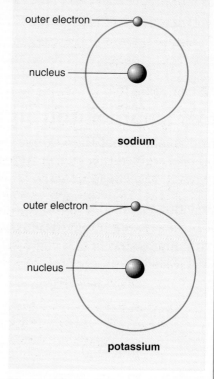

Figure 14 ▲

Summary

When you have finished studying this chapter, you should understand that:

✔ Most elements are metals.

✔ Metals vary in their reactivity.

✔ Some very unreactive metals are found as pure metals, however most metals are found as compounds with other elements.

✔ A list of metals in order of reactivity is called a reactivity series.

✔ Metals can be placed in the reactivity series depending on how easily they react with oxygen, water and dilute acids.

✔ More reactive metals displace less reactive metals from solution.

✔ The reactivity series can help you to choose the right metal for a particular purpose.

End-of-Chapter Questions

1 Explain in your own words the following key terms you have met in this chapter:

reactivity series

displacement reactions

galvanising

2 Imagine that a new metal has been discovered. It is given the name 'millennium'. Millennium is shiny and conducts heat well. It reacts with cold water to produce a gentle stream of gas bubbles. If a piece of millennium is placed in copper sulphate solution a pink solid is seen and the millennium slowly dissolves. A piece of zinc placed in millennium sulphate solution soon becomes covered with shiny crystals. Millennium burns brightly if heated in air, to form a white powder.

a) Apart from being shiny and conducting heat well, state two other properties which you would expect millennium to have.

b) What else would you expect to see when millennium was added to copper sulphate solution?

c) i) When millennium reacts with water, what gas do you think is formed?

ii) Suggest a word equation for the reaction.

iii) Assuming that millennium forms an ion with the symbol Mi^{2+}, write a symbol equation for the reaction of millennium with water.

d) i) What are the shiny crystals formed on the surface of the zinc?

ii) Write a chemical equation for their formation.

e) i) Place the elements copper, millennium and zinc in order of increasing reactivity, starting with the least reactive.

ii) Explain briefly how you arrived at this order of reactivity.

f) Name the 'white powder' formed when millennium burnt in air and write down its formula.

End-of-Chapter Questions continued

3 Sam's teacher told him that Galvani, an Italian scientist, had suggested that there would be a voltage between two different metals if they were in the same solution. Galvani also said that the voltage would be bigger the greater the difference in their reactivities. Sam decided to carry out some experiments to see if Galvani was correct. Sam's apparatus is shown in the diagram and his results are in the table.

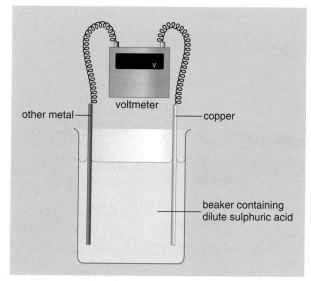

Other metal	Reading on voltmeter in V
iron	0.80
magnesium	2.70
aluminium	2.00
zinc	1.10

a) Do Sam's results support what Galvani said? Explain your answer.

b) Sam's teacher said that he should be suspicious about the result for aluminium. Why do you think the teacher said this?

c) Sam did two more experiments with other metals: nickel gave a voltage of 0.60 volts and tin gave a voltage of 0.50 volts. Put all six metals into a reactivity series, starting with the most reactive.

d) Both Sam's experiment and simply looking for signs of a reaction when one metal is added to a solution of a salt of another can both be used to set up a reactivity series. Discuss the advantages and disadvantages of the two methods.

4 From your knowledge of the reactivity series, state what you would expect to happen when:

a) zinc is heated with magnesium oxide

b) sodium is added to water

c) copper oxide is heated in a stream of hydrogen

d) aluminium powder and zinc oxide are heated together.

Write word and chemical equations for any reactions and if there is no reaction, explain why not.

11

Environmental chemistry

Could you tell where in the countryside you were by looking at the plants around you? Some plants, such as orchids, will only grow in soils rich in calcium and these are found mostly on chalk downs, which are well-drained and alkaline. Wet, acidic conditions, such as those found in bogs, favour the growth of heather, sedges and mosses. Extreme environments, such as those near the sea, are home to plants specially adapted to tolerate high levels of salt and these include the yellow-horned poppy and resistant grasses such as Sheep's Fescue.

Figure 1 ▲

What are soils?

In Chapter 7 we saw how rocks were broken down into smaller and smaller fragments by the processes of weathering. Over thousands of years, as weathering continues, rock gets broken down into smaller and smaller pieces so that, eventually, it becomes soil.

Soils consist of decomposed and fragmented rock, containing varying amounts of **humus**. Humus is a dark material formed from the decomposition of plant and animal matter.

The eventual properties of a soil depend on the following factors:

- the rock from which the soil was formed
- the climatic conditions
- how old the soil is
- the topography – whether the land is flat or sloping
- the plant and animal activity in the soil.

By volume, an average soil consists of:

- 45% minerals
- 25% water
- 25% air
- 5% organic matter (both living and dead organisms).

Soils have layers, called soil horizons, which show the various stages in the development of the soil. Only the top layer, supports plant growth.

Soil acidity

The acidity of soil is measured on the **pH scale**. The pH scale runs from pH 0 (very acidic) to pH 14 (very alkaline), with pH 7 being neutral (see Chapter 3).

Soils are naturally slightly acidic, this is because the carbon dioxide dissolved in rainwater makes it a very dilute acid.

$$\text{carbon dioxide} + \text{water} \rightarrow \text{carbonic acid}$$
$$CO_2 \qquad + H_2O \quad \rightarrow H_2CO_3$$

Most plants will grow well in a slightly acidic soil of pH 6.5, but different plants grow best in soils with a particular pH value.

Plant	Preferred pH
rhododendron, azaleas, ferns, coniferous trees	4.0–5.0
holly, oak, birch, willow	5.0–6.0
most vegetables and fruit	6.0–7.0
asparagus	7.0–8.0

Table 1 ▲

The pH of the soil affects the availability of the nutrients that plants need for healthy growth. The most important plant nutrients are nitrogen, phosphorus and potassium.

Table 2 shows how the availability of these nutrients is affected by the pH of the soil.

Nutrient	Most available in pH range
nitrogen	6.0–8.0
phosphorus	6.5–8.0
potassium	6.0–10.0

Table 2 ▲

If a soil is too acidic (pH less than 6.0), very little of these important nutrients will be available. If the pH is too high (pH greater than 8.0), all but potassium will become scarce.

Testing soil pH

As the pH of a soil is very important, we need a method of testing the pH of a soil. A sample of the soil is shaken with distilled water and the solid material allowed to settle. A few drops of universal indicator are then added to the solution and the pH is found by comparing the colour produced with a colour chart.

The pH of different parts of a particular patch of soil may vary quite a lot. In order to get an accurate value, the pH should be determined in several places and the average pH value taken.

Changing the pH of soil

Very few soils are too alkaline, but more and more soils are becoming too acid. This is because the carbon dioxide and sulphur dioxide produced when we burn fossil fuels, react with rainwater to produce acid rain. Therefore, we need ways of reducing the acidity of a soil.

To make the soil fertile, the acid in the soil must be neutralised by adding an alkali. Calcium hydroxide (lime) is a good alkali to choose. The calcium hydroxide reacts with the acids in the soil to produce a salt and water. This raises the pH of the soil to the neutral value of 7.

Test Yourself

6   Suggest why soils are generally more acidic today than they were a hundred years ago.

Test Yourself

1   List the factors that affect the eventual properties of a soil.

2   What is the best pH for healthy plant growth?

3   Name a plant that can grow well in an acidic soil.

4   Explain how the pH has an effect on how well plants grow.

Test Yourself

5   When testing the pH of a soil sample, why is solid material allowed to settle before the pH is measured?

Figure 2 ▼   This farmer is adding calcium hydroxide to the soil to make it less acidic

Rocks, soil and weathering

Chemical weathering is the wearing down of a rock by dissolving it away Chapter 7 (page 87).

Limestone (calcium carbonate) rocks are the most likely to be badly weathered, because they react easily with acids. Because rainwater is a weak acid (carbonic acid), it reacts with limestone. The carbonic acid dissolves solid calcium carbonate, carrying it away in solution as calcium hydrogencarbonate.

calcium carbonate + carbonic acid→ calcium hydrogencarbonate
                    (solid)   (in solution)

$$CaCO_3 \quad\quad + H_2CO_3 \quad\quad \rightarrow Ca(HCO_3)_2$$

Although carbonic acid is a very weak acid, over millions of years the action of water containing dissolved carbon dioxide has shaped the landscape, both above and below ground. This can be seen especially in areas where limestone is the dominant rock type.

Caves like the one shown in Figure 3 are formed because an underground river once flowed through the rock, carrying the limestone away in solution. Water draining down through the rock above the cave also contributed to making the amazing formations in the cave.

The water draining down through the cave contains a lot of dissolved calcium salts –which forms the stalactites, on the roof of the cave, and the stalagmites, on the floor of the cave. Each drop of water that falls from a stalactite leaves a minute deposit of calcium carbonate. When the drop hits the floor a corresponding stalagmite forms. You can see that some stalactites and stalagmites have met and formed pillars in the cave.

Acidic rainwater is at work above ground too; and again limestone is most at risk. Look at the limestone carvings in Figure 4. You can see that the older carving looks very different. Not only has it been damaged by weathering, but it is dirty because of the soot that comes out of the exhaust of vehicles and sticks to the stonework. The particles of soot and other solids from exhausts are called 'particulates'. Particulates can also damage our lungs if we breathe in too much of them.

Figure 3 ▲

Test Yourself

7   Explain in your own words how a stalactite is formed.

Figure 4 ▶   The limestone carvings on Wells Cathedral have been badly damaged by acid rain, so they are now being replaced by new carvings like the one on the left

a)

b)

Figure 5 ▲

Factors affecting weathering

Generally, weathering is most rapid when rainfall is acidic (has a low pH) and where there is a high annual rainfall.

The photographs in Figure 5 show two buildings, one in the Egyptian desert, which gets hardly any rain, and one in London. Both buildings are made of limestone – can you notice a difference?

Air pollution

The invention of the internal combustion engine, which is used in motor cars and lorries, and the increasing use of fossil fuels to heat our homes and to generate electricity have increased **air pollution**. Air pollution means that substances have been added to the atmosphere that are not present naturally or, that substances have been added in greater amounts than normally present.

The major pollutant from fossil fuels is carbon dioxide; we shall consider its effect on the environment later (see page 158). As well as carbon dioxide, the burning of fossil fuels also puts more sulphur dioxide and nitrogen oxides into the atmosphere. These also have an effect on the environment.

Sulphur dioxide

All fossil fuels contain some sulphur. When the sulphur is burnt with the fuel it forms sulphur dioxide:

$$\text{sulphur} + \text{oxygen} \rightarrow \text{sulphur dioxide}$$
$$\text{S} + \text{O}_2 \rightarrow \text{SO}_2$$

(Note how sulphur dioxide is named. The '-oxide' part tells you that the sulphur has reacted with oxygen. The 'di-' part tells you that two oxygen atoms join to each sulphur atom. This is shown in the chemical formula, which is SO_2.)

The sulphur dioxide rises into the atmosphere and dissolves in rainwater. Sulphur dioxide makes the rainwater much more acidic than carbon dioxide does. Sulphur dioxide is also much more soluble in water. We call rainwater containing sulphur dioxide **acid rain**.

$$\text{sulphur dioxide} + \text{water} \rightarrow \text{sulphurous acid}$$
$$SO_2 + H_2O \rightarrow H_2SO_3$$

High in the atmosphere, sulphur dioxide can react with more oxygen to give sulphur trioxide.

$$\text{sulphur dioxide} + \text{oxygen} \rightarrow \text{sulphur trioxide}$$
$$2SO_2 + O_2 \rightarrow 2SO_3$$

(Sulphur trioxide has three oxygen atoms attached to each sulphur atom – three is 'tri-', as in 'triangle'.)

Sulphur trioxide dissolves in water to give sulphuric acid, which is a stronger acid than sulphurous acid and does much more damage.

$$\text{sulphur trioxide} + \text{water} \rightarrow \text{sulphuric acid}$$
$$SO_3 + H_2O \rightarrow H_2SO_4$$

To help to reduce emissions of sulphur dioxide, fuels can have the sulphur removed from them. These fuels are called **desulphurised fuels**. Most petrol stations now sell low sulphur petrol and low sulphur diesel and desulphurised coal has been used in American cities for over 40 years.

Volcanic eruptions are natural sources of sulphur dioxide and carbon dioxide, which put millions of tonnes of these gases into the atmosphere each year. However, the amount of sulphur dioxide and carbon dioxide produced by burning fossil fuels, i.e. produced artificially, is far greater (Table 3). An additional problem with fossil fuels is that they are burned where people are most concentrated – in towns and cities. This means that the sulphur dioxide produced is an even greater threat to human health.

Test Yourself

8 What is the main substance that dissolves in rainwater to make it acidic?

9 Explain how this substance gets into the atmosphere.

10 What steps might be taken to reduce emissions of this substance into the atmosphere?

11 Why is atmospheric pollution a greater problem in cities than in the countryside?

	Artificial	Natural
amount of sulphur dioxide produced in millions of tonnes per year	190	1–50
amount of carbon dioxide produced in millions of tonnes per year	30 000	65–500

Table 3 ▲ A comparison of the sources of sulphur dioxide and carbon dioxide

Nitrogen oxides

When fuels burn, oxygen combines with the substances in the fuel, forming new substances and giving out energy. High temperatures are generated when fuels burn. These high temperatures allow the nitrogen in the air to react with the oxygen to give nitrogen oxides. Large amounts of nitrogen oxides are produced by cars.

The first nitrogen oxide to form is called nitrogen monoxide:

$$\text{nitrogen} + \text{oxygen} \rightarrow \text{nitrogen monoxide}$$
$$N_2 + O_2 \rightarrow 2NO$$

(The 'mono-' in nitrogen monoxide shows that one oxygen atom is attached to the nitrogen atom.)

This reaction also takes place in thunderstorms, because the lightning flashes generate the high temperatures needed. Rain which falls during thunderstorms is more acidic than rain which falls when there is no lightning.

Nitrogen monoxide then reacts with more oxygen to give nitrogen dioxide:

$$\text{nitrogen monoxide} + \text{oxygen} \rightarrow \text{nitrogen dioxide}$$
$$2NO + O_2 \rightarrow 2NO_2$$

The nitrogen dioxide then passes into the atmosphere in the exhaust gases from the vehicle.

In a similar way to sulphur dioxide, nitrogen dioxide reacts with water in the presence of oxygen to form an acid, called nitric acid.

$$\text{nitrogen dioxide} + \text{oxygen} + \text{water} \rightarrow \text{nitric acid}$$
$$4NO_2 + O_2 + 2H_2O \rightarrow 4HNO_3$$

Reducing pollution caused by nitrogen oxides

Reducing the pollution caused by sulphur dioxide is quite easy – the sulphur can be removed from the fuels we burn. Reducing the pollution caused by nitrogen oxides is more difficult. There is no way of preventing a mixture of nitrogen and oxygen from reacting when fossil fuels are burned – both the gases are present in air.

The solution is to use a **catalytic converter** and make the exhaust gases pass over the catalysts. In the catalytic converter, harmful nitrogen oxides are converted back to nitrogen. Catalytic converters also reduce the levels of other pollutants from the exhaust, such as unburnt fuel and carbon monoxide.

Test Yourself

12 Explain how nitrogen oxides are formed in a car engine.

13 Why is it more difficult to control the level of nitrogen oxides in the atmosphere than it is to control the level of other polluting gases?

Extension box

Catalytic converters

The main pollutants derived from vehicle engines are:

- nitrogen oxides, produced from oxygen and nitrogen reacting at the high temperature in the engine
- carbon monoxide, produced from the incomplete combustion of fuel
- unburnt fuel, which is a mixture of hydrocarbons.

There are three pollutants to deal with, so most vehicles use a 'three-way' catalytic converter.

The reduction catalyst

At the heart of a catalytic converter used in a car is a ceramic honeycomb that has a high melting point. The honeycomb is coated with the metal catalysts. The reduction catalyst is a mixture of two expensive metals, platinum and rhodium. You can see the ceramic honeycomb and the metal coating in Figure 6. This method of construction gives the catalyst the largest possible surface area and so cuts down on the amount of the expensive metals needed.

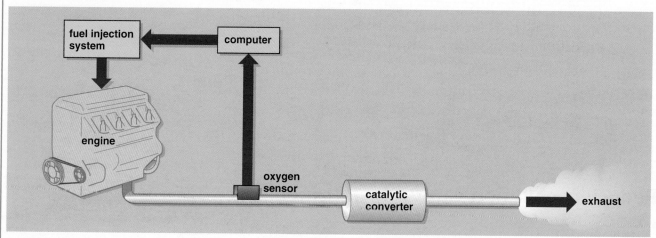

Figure 6

The reduction catalyst reduces the amount of nitrogen oxides in the exhaust by converting them into harmless nitrogen and oxygen.

For nitrogen dioxide:

$$2NO_2 \rightarrow N_2 + 2O_2$$

For nitrogen monoxide:

$$2NO \rightarrow N_2 + O_2$$

Extension box continued

The oxidation catalyst

The oxygen formed in the reduction catalyst is used in the oxidation catalyst to reduce the amount of carbon monoxide and unburnt fuel in the exhaust.

Carbon monoxide is oxidised to carbon dioxide:

$$2CO + O_2 \rightarrow 2CO_2$$

Unburnt fuel (represented here by octane, C_8H_{18}) is oxidised to carbon dioxide and water:

$$C_8H_{18} + 12\tfrac{1}{2}O_2 \rightarrow 8CO_2 + 9H_2O$$

The oxygen sensor and engine management computer

Between the engine and the catalytic converter is an oxygen sensor. This detects how much oxygen there is in the exhaust and feeds the result to a computer that is linked to the engine's fuel injection system. The fuel injection system ensures that there is the right amount of oxygen to burn the fuel as efficiently as possible, ensuring maximum engine power and a minimum of pollution.

The fuel injection system also allows for the fact that some oxygen needs to be left over so that the carbon monoxide and any fuel that fails to burn in the engine can be removed in the oxidation catalyst.

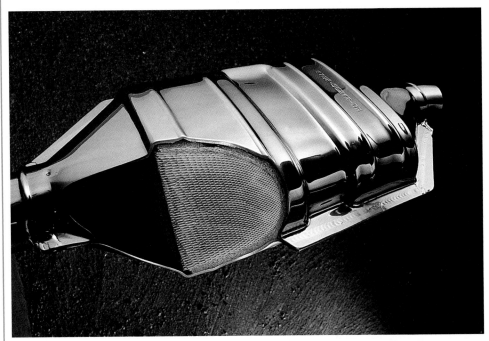

Figure 7 ▲   A catalytic converter

Extension box continued

Unleaded petrol and the catalytic converter

Lead compounds used to be added to petrol to make engines work more efficiently. The lead compounds were burned in the engine and then came out of the exhaust as lead compounds. Lead compounds are poisonous and the levels of lead pollution near roads became very high. Young children were especially at risk – the worry was that the high levels of lead reduced mental ability.

During the 1970s, compounds were invented which had the same effect as the lead compounds in improving engine efficiency, but had no pollution problems. Lead is no longer added to petrol. Vehicles fitted with catalytic converters cannot use leaded petrol because the lead compounds cover the surface of the catalyst. Lead is said to 'poison' the catalyst by stopping the exhaust gases from reaching the catalyst.

Test Yourself

14 Why is the catalyst in a catalytic converter made in the form of a honeycomb?

15 Explain why leaded petrol cannot be used in vehicles fitted with a catalytic converter.

The effects of acid rain

The three acids formed as a result of burning fossil fuels are sulphurous acid, sulphuric acid and nitric acid. These three acids increase the acidity of rain much more than carbonic acid.

Figure 8 ◄ These trees have been damaged by acid rain

The effects of acid rain are the following:

- damages the surface of building stone, causing the stone to break up
- destroys the detail on stone carvings and inscriptions
- increases the rate of rusting of iron
- corrodes the steel reinforcing rods used in concrete
- makes soils acidic so plants cannot get the nutrients they need
- washes essential metals, such as magnesium and aluminium, out of the soil
- damages the leaves of plants
- makes it easier for plants to take up toxic metals from the soil
- lakes become more acidic and some organisms die as a result
- toxic heavy metals are washed out of the soil into lakes and these can kill fish.

Test Yourself

16 List four effects of acid rain.

Monitoring air pollution

It is impossible to obtain air that is completely free of pollution. The pollutants in the air cannot be removed and the rapid movement and diffusion of the particles in a gas means that the pollutants mix completely with the air. The realistic view is to set maximum limits on the concentration of each air pollutant, based on what is known about the effects of each pollutant on health and on the environment. These maximum concentration limits are called air quality standards. They can be used as a guide to see if air pollution is increasing or decreasing.

The standards adopted in the UK are the National Air Quality Standards, part of the National Air Quality Strategy adopted by the Government in January 2000. Some of these standards are given in Table 4.

Pollutant	Concentration	Measured as
carbon monoxide	10 ppm (11.6 mg/m^3)	8 hour mean
nitrogen dioxide	150 ppb (287 µg/m^3)	1 hour mean
sulphur dioxide	100 ppb (266 µg/m^3)	15 minute mean
sulphur dioxide	8 ppb (20 µg/m^3)	annual mean

Table 4 ▲
A concentration of 1 ppm (1 part per million) corresponds to 1 cm^3 of the pollutant in every cubic metre of air. A concentration of 1 ppb (1 part per billion) corresponds to 1 mm^3 of the pollutant in every cubic metre of air

You will see that it is possible to have both long-term and short-term limits; for sulphur dioxide no-one should be exposed to more than 100 ppb (parts per billion) for 15 minutes and their annual exposure should not exceed 8 ppb.

The difficult issue in pollution is that of long-term exposure. Anyone exposed to high concentrations of sulphur dioxide will experience its ill-effects straight away – a choking sensation and eye irritation. It is very difficult to predict the effects of long-term exposure to low levels of any pollutant. Any damage done may only become apparent a long time later, when the link between the pollutant and its effects is not obvious.

Information on air quality in the UK is available on the UK National Air Quality Information Archive (http://www.aeat.co.uk/netcen/airqual/home.html).

How is air pollution monitored?

Most air pollution is monitored by static monitoring stations situated strategically to give a good average picture of the situation throughout the country. Because most pollution is associated with vehicles or with industry, urban areas will usually have more monitoring stations than might be found in the countryside.

The map in Figure 9 shows the location of the automatic monitoring network in the UK for sulphur dioxide. There are other networks for ozone, nitrogen dioxide, carbon monoxide, particulates and hydrocarbons.

How is the level of pollution measured?

There are three methods of measuring levels of pollution:

- passive sampling methods
- active sampling methods
- automatic sampling methods.

Passive sampling

Passive sampling methods are a simple and cheap method of monitoring pollution levels. A plastic tube containing a chemical which absorbs the pollutant is left for between a week and a month in the location being monitored. Air diffuses into the tube and the pollutants are absorbed by the chemical. The tube is then collected and taken back to the laboratory for analysis.

Test Yourself

17 What is the difference between a long-term effect and a short-term effect of a pollutant?

Test Yourself

18 Suggest why the pollution monitoring stations shown in Figure 9 are distributed the way they are.

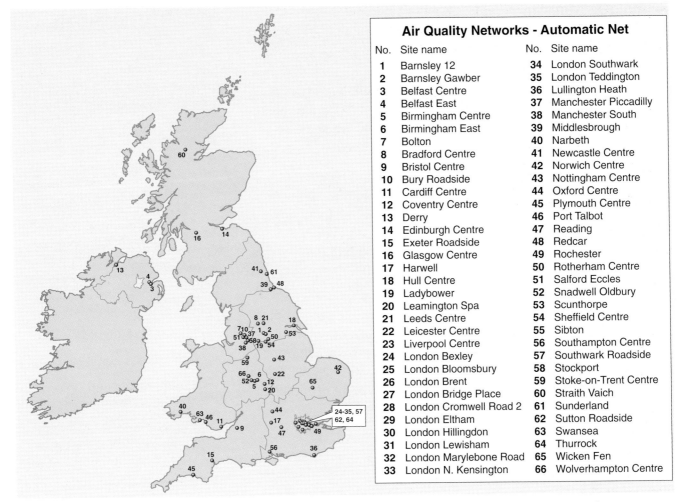

Air Quality Networks - Automatic Net

No.	Site name	No.	Site name
1	Barnsley 12	34	London Southwark
2	Barnsley Gawber	35	London Teddington
3	Belfast Centre	36	Lullington Heath
4	Belfast East	37	Manchester Piccadilly
5	Birmingham Centre	38	Manchester South
6	Birmingham East	39	Middlesbrough
7	Bolton	40	Narbeth
8	Bradford Centre	41	Newcastle Centre
9	Bristol Centre	42	Norwich Centre
10	Bury Roadside	43	Nottingham Centre
11	Cardiff Centre	44	Oxford Centre
12	Coventry Centre	45	Plymouth Centre
13	Derry	46	Port Talbot
14	Edinburgh Centre	47	Reading
15	Exeter Roadside	48	Redcar
16	Glasgow Centre	49	Rochester
17	Harwell	50	Rotherham Centre
18	Hull Centre	51	Salford Eccles
19	Ladybower	52	Snadwell Oldbury
20	Leamington Spa	53	Scunthorpe
21	Leeds Centre	54	Sheffield Centre
22	Leicester Centre	55	Sibton
23	Liverpool Centre	56	Southampton Centre
24	London Bexley	57	Southwark Roadside
25	London Bloomsbury	58	Stockport
26	London Brent	59	Stoke-on-Trent Centre
27	London Bridge Place	60	Straith Vaich
28	London Cromwell Road 2	61	Sunderland
29	London Eltham	62	Sutton Roadside
30	London Hillingdon	63	Swansea
31	London Lewisham	64	Thurrock
32	London Marylebone Road	65	Wicken Fen
33	London N. Kensington	66	Wolverhampton Centre

Figure 9 ▲ Air quality monitoring stations in the UK

Because this method is cheap it is possible to place a large number of tubes in a particular area and this allows areas of particularly high pollution to be investigated (perhaps near a motorway or a factory). Such an investigation could lead to a more detailed study by other methods. The disadvantage of passive sampling is that a comparatively small volume of air is sampled, so low concentrations of pollutants may not show up. It is also not very easy to work out just what volume of air diffused into the tube during its exposure.

Active sampling

An alternative is to use active sampling methods. In active sampling methods a known volume of air is pumped for a known length of time through a filter or a chemical to absorb the pollutant. The sample is then removed for analysis in the laboratory.

The analysis takes a shorter time than for passive sampling, so samples can be taken every day. This can be useful, for example if you wanted to know how pollution from vehicle exhausts varies during the week.

Automatic sampling

Automatic sampling methods differ from the other two methods, because the analysis is done continuously in real time and the results are relayed back to computers in the laboratory. Analysis can be carried out over short time periods, so the variation in concentration of a pollutant during the rush hour could easily be measured. The results are much more accurate, but the cost of the equipment and the need to maintain it to a high standard make this method expensive.

Test Yourself

19 List the three methods of pollution monitoring, giving an advantage and a disadvantage of each method.

Water quality

The composition of water around the country differs much more than the air. This is because water carries with it minerals picked up from the rocks over which it has passed.

Drinking water is obtained from a wide variety of sources, but it is all treated in the same way. The water is filtered to make it clear by removing suspended matter. It is treated with chlorine to kill harmful bacteria. Although the minerals in drinking water will depend on where the water came from originally, all drinking water must:

- be free of colour
- have no odour
- not contain suspended matter
- be free of bacteria.

The same three general methods of analysis used to assess air quality can also be used for water.

Global warming

Carbon dioxide gas is harmless to humans in the concentrations found in the atmosphere. However, many scientists believe that carbon dioxide is affecting our climate. Table 5 shows some predictions that have been made concerning **global warming**, together with the actual outcome.

Looking at a wider range of predictions, an American scientist called Douglas Hoyt found that of 33 predictions about global warming only 5 turned out to be correct. One set of temperature measurements he looked at actually showed a fall in temperature between 1955 and 1990 of 0.6 °C, compared to a predicted increase of 1.6 °C.

Event	Prediction	Outcome	Right or wrong?
1830–1997 surface temperature trend	0.6 to 1.8 °C warming	little warming, perhaps 0.1 to 0.2 °C due to greenhouse gases	✗
1940–1997 surface temperature trend	0.3 to 0.9 °C warming	no statistically significant warming (GISS and CRU), but a warming of 0.2 °C can be claimed	✗
1979–1997 surface temperature trend	about a 0.3 °C warming per decade	0.1 °C warming per decade	✗
1940–1997 surface temperature trend in Arctic regions	1.0 to 3.0 °C warming	a definite cooling trend since 1940. July 1997 was the coldest month ever observed in Antarctica	✗
Northern Hemisphere snow and ice cover	decreasing	decreasing	✔
Mountain glaciers	receding	receding in eight mountain ranges. Advancing in three mountain ranges	✔

Table 5 ▲

There is no doubt that greenhouse gases, such as carbon dioxide, do cause an increase in the Earth's mean temperature. However, it is far from clear that they are the major factor in global warming.

The following news report from the BBC in 1998 gives another view of the problem.

Scientists blame Sun for global warming

The Sun is more active than it has ever been in the last 300 years. Climate changes such as global warming may be due to changes in the Sun rather than to the release of greenhouse gases on Earth.

Climatologists and astronomers speaking at the American Association for the Advancement of Science meeting in Philadelphia say the present warming may be unusual – but a mini ice age could soon follow.

The Sun provides all the energy that drives our climate, but it is not the constant star it might seem. Careful studies over the last 20 years show that its overall brightness and energy output increases slightly as sunspot activity rises to the peak of its 11-year cycle.

continued ▶▶

And individual cycles can be more or less active. The Sun is currently at its most active for 300 years. That, say scientists in Philadelphia, could be a more significant cause of global warming than the emissions of greenhouse gases that are most often blamed.

The researchers point out that much of the half-a-degree rise in global temperature over the last 120 years occurred before 1940 – earlier than the biggest rise in greenhouse gas emissions.

Ancient trees reveal most warm spells are caused by the Sun. Using ancient tree rings, they show that 17 out of 19 warm spells in the last 10, 000 years coincided with peaks in solar activity.

They have also studied other Sun-like stars and found that they spend significant periods without sunspots at all, so perhaps cool spells should be feared more than global warming.

The scientists do not pretend they can explain everything, nor do they say that attempts to reduce greenhouse gas emissions should be abandoned. But they do feel that understanding of our nearest star must be increased if the climate is to be understood.

The greenhouse effect

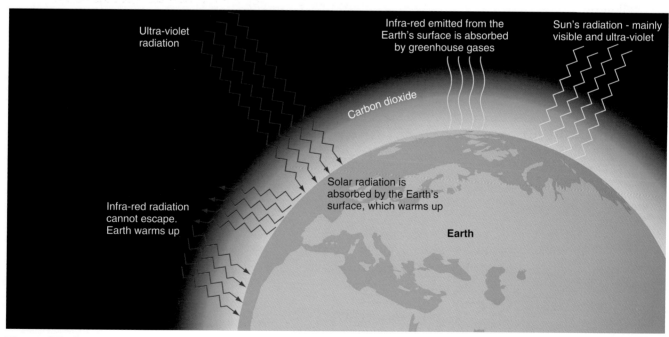

Ultra-violet radiation

Infra-red emitted from the Earth's surface is absorbed by greenhouse gases

Sun's radiation - mainly visible and ultra-violet

Carbon dioxide

Infra-red radiation cannot escape. Earth warms up

Solar radiation is absorbed by the Earth's surface, which warms up

Earth

Figure 10 ▲

Apart from light energy from the Sun, a lot of ultraviolet radiation reaches the Earth through the atmosphere. This ultraviolet radiation warms the surface of the Earth. Infrared radiation (heat energy) is given off from the Earth but cannot escape back through the atmosphere because **greenhouse gases** such as carbon dioxide and water vapour trap it – this leads to the **greenhouse effect**. The greater the amount of carbon dioxide in the atmosphere, the more heat is prevented from escaping and the hotter the Earth gets.

The increased amounts of fossil fuels burnt has increased the amount of carbon dioxide in the atmosphere. Carbon dioxide has always been a part of the atmosphere; some scientists say we should be talking about the 'enhanced' greenhouse effect when we consider the effects of fossil fuels on the environment.

Summary

When you have finished studying this chapter, you should understand that:

✔ Soils form when small rock fragments mix with organic matter.

✔ Slightly alkaline soils are best for plant growth.

✔ Acidic soil can be treated to make them alkaline.

✔ Weathering causes rocks to dissolve and wear away.

✔ Acid rain from polluted air increases the weathering of rocks.

✔ The burning of fossil fuels is partly responsible for acid rain.

✔ Nitrogen oxides also produce acid rain.

✔ Catalytic converters in vehicles cut down emissions of nitrogen oxides.

✔ Air pollution is regularly monitored.

✔ The Earth's temperature seems to be increasing gradually.

✔ The greenhouse effect is responsible for part of this temperature rise.

End-of-Chapter Questions

1 Explain in your own words the following key terms you have met in this chapter:

humus

pH scale

chemical weathering

air pollution

acid rain

desulphurised fuels

catalytic converter

global warming

greenhouse gases

greenhouse effect

2 The pH of some soil samples from five locations are shown below.

Location	pH
A	9.0
B	6.5
C	7.0
D	4.0
E	3.0

a) What does the pH of the soil measure?

b) i) In which location is the soil most acidic?

ii) How might an acidic soil be made less acidic? What would happen to its pH when this was done?

iii) The acidic location is downwind of a large factory. What might be emitted from the factory to make the soil acidic? Why is it significant that the location is downwind of the factory?

c) In which location is the soil likely to have been formed from limestone rocks? Explain your answer.

3 Plants need several nutrients for healthy growth. The diagram below shows the relationship between soil pH and the availability of some of these nutrients. The wider the bar, the more available the nutrient.

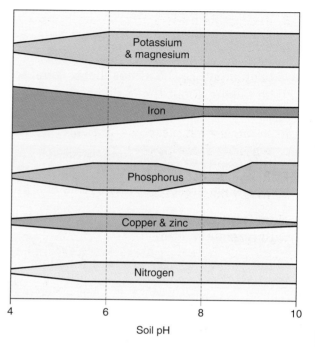

a) For which two nutrients is their availability least affected by soil pH?

b) i) Which nutrient has the highest availability in acidic soils?

ii) Plants do not generally grow well in acidic soils. Suggest why.

c) Which pH seems best to ensure the maximum availability of all of the nutrients shown?

d) Which two nutrients become less available in both acidic and alkaline soils?

e) A farmer wants to grow crops in a soil containing a lot of limestone. What two nutrients might he have to add to ensure that his crops grow well?

End-of-Chapter Questions continued

4 Fred decided to carry out some experiments to see whether different kinds of rock weathered at the same rate. His experimental plan was as follows.

A Take pieces of rock of equal mass and as nearly as possible the same shape.

B Record the mass of each piece of rock.

C Place each piece in a beaker of dilute hydrochloric acid of the same concentration.

D Leave the pieces in the acid for a week.

E Remove each piece, wash it with distilled water and dry it.

F Re-weigh each piece and work out how much mass it has lost.

Here are his results:

Sample	Loss in mass in grams
1	10.3
2	0.5
3	4.1
4	1.3

a) State three steps that were taken to ensure that the test was fair.

b) Explain which sample was most likely to be a limestone rock.

c) In what ways does Fred's experiment differ from the way rocks are weathered in the environment?

d) How might Fred's experiment have been modified to see whether:

   i)   the temperature or

   ii) the availability of air

affected the rate of weathering?

5 The diagram below shows three experiments to study the effect of sulphur dioxide on three identical samples of limestone.

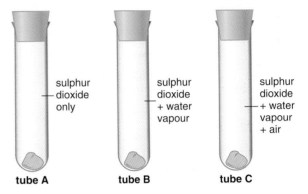

sulphur dioxide only   sulphur dioxide + water vapour   sulphur dioxide + water vapour + air

tube A   tube B   tube C

The tubes were filled as shown and left for a week in the laboratory.

a) After this time, the limestone in tube A showed no signs of reaction. Suggest an explanation.

b) The limestone in tube B showed signs of reaction, but far less than the limestone in tube C. Explain these observations.

6 Plots of the sulphur dioxide concentration at a roadside site in London at various times of the day in 1976 and 1996 are shown below. Note that the concentrations are plotted on different scales.

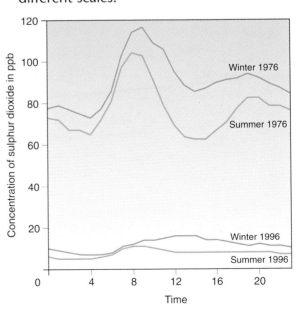

End-of-Chapter Questions continued

a) i) What is the main source of sulphur dioxide pollution?

   ii) Describe the chemical reactions that take place once sulphur dioxide reaches the atmosphere. What is eventually formed as a result of these reactions?

   iii) Explain how sulphur dioxide emissions can affect the environment.

b) Suggest why the concentration of sulphur dioxide is greater in the winter than in the summer.

c) The 1976 figures show high concentrations of sulphur dioxide at around 08:00 and 20:00 hours. Suggest a reason for these high concentrations.

d) Suggest reasons for the reduction in the concentration of sulphur dioxide over the period 1976 to 1996.

7 The graph shows the changes in the mean annual concentration of nitrogen oxides in central London for the period 1990 to 1999. Motor vehicle exhausts are the main source of pollution by nitrogen oxides.

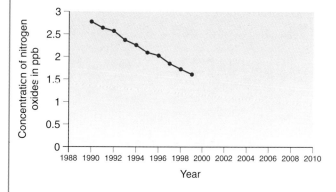

a) i) Explain why oxides of nitrogen are found in the exhaust of motor vehicles.

   ii) What advance in vehicle exhaust systems has helped to reduce pollution by oxides of nitrogen? Explain how this advance works.

   iii) Explain why a change in petrol additives was needed to allow this advance to be successful.

b) i) Considering the trend shown from 1990 to 1999, predict what you would expect the concentration of nitrogen oxides to be in the year 2009.

   ii) Discuss the factors that might make your prediction inaccurate.

8 The graphs below show the daily changes in carbon monoxide concentration at the same site for 1972 and 1992.

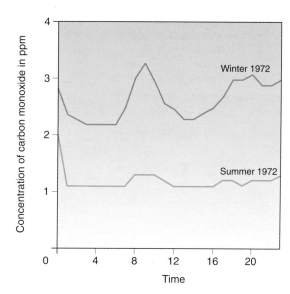

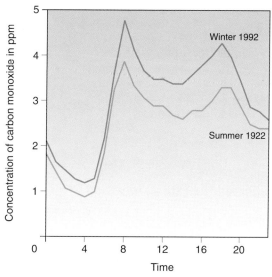

End-of-Chapter Questions continued

a) Explain the general shape of the winter plots for both years.

b) i)   What has been the general trend in the level of carbon monoxide pollution from 1972 to 1992?

ii)   Discuss the factors that have contributed to this trend.

c) Suggest why the winter level of carbon monoxide pollution is always greater than the summer level.

9 Discuss the advantages and disadvantages of the following as fuels:

- ethanol, a renewable fuel obtained from sugar cane by fermentation (See page 25, Chapter 2)

- hydrogen, obtainable from water by electrolysis (See page 169, Chapter 12)

- petrol, obtained from crude oil.

    You should consider the ease of obtaining the fuel, the problems in using and handling it, and its effect on the environment.

10 a) Explain what is meant by the term 'greenhouse gases'.

b) Explain the effects of greenhouse gases on the environment.

c) Can global warming be blamed on these gases entirely?

12 Using chemistry

In this chapter you will learn about the ways in which we have used chemistry to make our lives easier. Portable electrical devices, such as torches, radios, minidisk players and mobile telephones have made our lives safer, more convenient and fun – but are only made possible by the invention of the battery.

Advances in our ability to make new materials economically and on a large scale have given us fertilisers to improve crop yields, which has meant a better-fed world.

Figure 1 ▼

Fossil fuels

Fossil fuels were created millions of years ago from the remains of dead animals and plants. The three main fossil fuels are coal, oil and natural gas.

- Coal was used a lot to heat homes, but it is less popular these days. It is still burned in large quantities in power stations to generate electricity.
- Oil is the source material for useful fuels such as petrol and diesel, as well as lots of other materials, such as plastics.
- Natural gas, which is mainly methane, is used in the home for central heating and for cooking.

Oil and natural gas are mixtures of compounds containing only the elements carbon and hydrogen – they are called **hydrocarbon fuels**.

What makes a good fuel?

Almost anything can be burned, but that does not make everything a good fuel. A good fuel should:

- be plentiful
- be cheap
- give out a lot of energy when it burns
- produce as little pollution as possible.

When fuels containing carbon and hydrogen burn, the products formed depend on the amount of oxygen available to burn the fuel.

If there is plenty of oxygen, then water and carbon dioxide are formed.

$$\text{methane} + \text{oxygen} \rightarrow \text{water} + \text{carbon dioxide}$$
$$CH_4 + 2O_2 \rightarrow 2H_2O + CO_2$$

If there isn't enough oxygen to burn the fuel completely, poisonous carbon monoxide can be formed, as well as soot. This is known as **incomplete combustion**. You may have seen the effect of incomplete combustion in the laboratory when using a Bunsen burner. When a beaker of water is heated using a blue Bunsen flame – in which the methane is being burned completely – there is no soot on the bottom of the beaker. If a yellow flame is used, however, the methane is not completely burned and you see soot collecting on the bottom of the beaker.

You often see soot inside a car exhaust pipe. This will happen where the petrol hasn't been burned in enough oxygen. Diesel engines make most soot and you can often see clouds of soot when lorries or buses move off.

$$\text{methane} + \text{oxygen} \rightarrow \text{water} + \text{carbon (soot)}$$
$$CH_4 + O_2 \rightarrow 2H_2O + C$$

Another problem of incomplete combustion is the formation of poisonous carbon monoxide. Carbon monoxide is very poisonous to animals because it stops the blood carrying oxygen around the body. Carbon monoxide isn't a problem in the open air, however, it is very dangerous to run a car engine in a closed garage because carbon monoxide can build up. Faulty gas heaters or boilers can produce dangerous amounts of carbon monoxide; it is important to have appliances checked regularly to make sure they are working properly.

$$\text{methane} + \text{oxygen} \rightarrow \text{water} + \text{carbon monoxide}$$
$$CH_4 + 1\tfrac{1}{2}O_2 \rightarrow 2H_2O + CO$$

Test Yourself

1   Suggest why natural gas is a more popular fuel than coal.

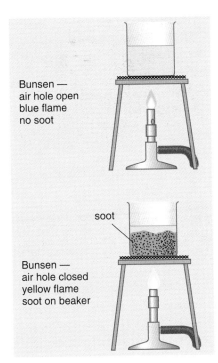

Bunsen — air hole open blue flame no soot

soot

Bunsen — air hole closed yellow flame soot on beaker

Figure 2 ▲   Incomplete combustion of methane produces soot

Incomplete combustion is undesirable:

- you get less energy from the fuel than if it burns completely
- carbon monoxide is poisonous
- soot makes the environment dirty
- soot can also cause illness if it is breathed in.

Choosing a hydrocarbon fuel

Some properties of the most important hydrocarbon fuels are shown in Table 1.

Name	Chemical formula	Boiling point in °C	Physical state at room temperature	Uses
methane	CH_4	−162	gas	domestic heating
propane	C_3H_8	−42	gas	blowtorches
butane	C_4H_{10}	−0.5	gas	camping stoves
petrol	$C_5H_{12} - C_{10}H_{22}$	about 120	liquid	petrol engines
diesel	$C_{15}H_{32} - C_{19}H_{40}$	about 300	liquid	diesel engines

Table 1 ▲

Methane, propane and butane are all good fuels. However, they all have one disadvantage – they are gases. Gases diffuse to fill all the space available to them, so if they are to be used as fuels they must be completely enclosed. The usual solution is to compress the gas into cylinders so that it liquefies under pressure. You then get more of the fuel in a given volume. If you simply filled a cylinder with the gas, there wouldn't be enough fuel to make it useful.

Methane has such a low boiling point that a cylinder strong enough to contain it as a liquid would be very heavy. Instead, methane is delivered to the point of use through a pipe; this is how natural gas arrives at your house. Propane and butane are not good fuels for cars, compared to petrol, because of the risk of explosion if the gas cylinders were damaged in an accident. Also, it would be more difficult to refuel a car with a gaseous fuel than with a liquid such as petrol or diesel.

Test Yourself

2   Design a poster illustrating as many disadvantages of incomplete combustion of petrol as you can.

Test Yourself

3   List the advantages and disadvantages of a liquid hydrocarbon fuel compared to a gaseous hydrocarbon fuel.

Hydrogen as a fuel

Many scientists think that hydrogen may be the fuel of the future, if and when oil supplies have run out. Hydrogen can be made from coal, which is still quite plentiful, or from water. Hydrogen has a big advantage over fossil fuels because it gives no carbon dioxide or soot when it burns, only water. The water formed is easy to condense and need not be allowed to pollute the atmosphere.

Ideas and Evidence

The Hindenberg problem

The major obstacle to using hydrogen as a fuel is that the general public considers hydrogen to be dangerous. This is a result of an accident to the airship *Hindenburg* on Thursday, May 6, 1937. The *Hindenburg* had flown from Germany but it exploded as it was landing in Lakelurst, New Jersey causing the loss of 36 lives (there were 97 people on board in all).

Despite the fact that it was later shown that it was the casing of the Hindenburg which had first caught fire, not the hydrogen, the event was so public and so awful that hydrogen has never shaken off the 'dangerous' label. Most of the fire damage was not caused by hydrogen, but by the diesel fuel that powered the engines. As Figure 3 shows, the flames from hydrogen burn upwards and away very quickly.

Figure 3 ◄

Advantages	Disadvantages
• does not pollute the atmosphere when it burns • weighs much less than petrol • will not spill like petrol (it instantly turns to a gas)	• needs a special insulated storage tank for the liquid • more difficult to refuel vehicles and it takes longer • greater cost (at present anyway)

Table 2 ▲   Considering hydrogen as a fuel

Batteries

Alessandro Volta

Count Alessandro Volta (1745–1827) was an Italian physicist who became particularly interested in electricity following a discovery by his friend, Luigi Galvani (see page 115, Chapter 9). Galvani noticed that the muscle from a frog's leg twitched when it was in contact with two different metals. Galvani decided that this was due to electricity that had come from the muscle. He called this 'animal electricity'. Volta was convinced that it was the metals and not the muscle that gave rise to the electric current. In 1794 he began a series of experiments with different metals, but without the muscle, and discovered that he could still produce electricity.

Volta replaced the muscle with discs of cardboard wetted with salt solution, placed between alternating discs of silver or copper and zinc. He literally made a pile of these discs and the invention became known as a 'voltaic pile'. There is a story that he persuaded a friendly bishop to let him use his cathedral tower to make the pile as high as he could.

Volta found that any two different metals separated by his discs of cardboard soaked in salt solution gave a voltage. An electric current flowed when the two ends of the voltaic pile were connected with a wire.

Figure 4 shows how electricity can be made using copper and zinc and a beaker of acid. Any two different metals will work, but the further apart the metals are in the reactivity series the bigger voltage you get. What happens is that electrons move from the more reactive metal, through the wire, to the less reactive metal. Reactive metals give up their electrons more easily. See Chapter 10 (page 130) for more details about the reactivity series.

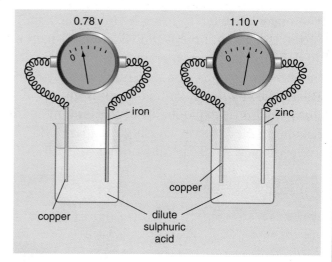

Figure 4 ▲

Test Yourself

6   How can you tell from the diagram that electricity has been produced?

7   How could you make the voltage larger?

You looked at displacement reactions in Chapter 10 (page 136). You can easily show that displacement reactions give out energy, in the form of heat energy, by adding some zinc powder to copper sulphate solution, stirring the mixture and watching the temperature rise.

You don't get enough heat energy in this experiment to make the reaction useful as a source of heat, but it can be used to make another form of energy – electricity.

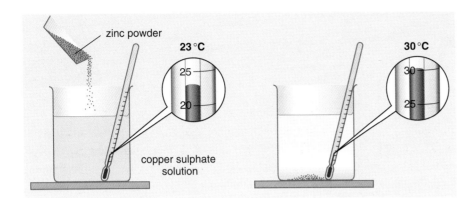

Figure 5 ◄ Displacement reactions give out heat

The following reaction takes place between zinc and copper sulphate:

zinc + copper sulphate → copper + zinc sulphate
$Zn(s) + CuSO_4(aq)$ → $Cu(s)$ + $ZnSO_4(aq)$

The zinc gradually goes into solution, pink copper metal appears and the blue colour of the copper sulphate solution fades.

Extension box

The chemistry of the reaction

During the displacement reaction, copper ions are converted to copper metal. To do this, copper ions must gain electrons:

copper ions + electrons → copper metal

$$Cu^{2+} + 2e^- \rightarrow Cu$$

At the same time, zinc metal loses electrons and dissolves as zinc ions:

zinc metal → zinc ions + electrons

$$Zn \rightarrow Zn^{2+} + 2e^-$$

Putting these two reactions together we get the equation for the chemical reaction taking place during the displacement reaction:

$$Cu^{2+} + Zn \rightarrow Cu + Zn^{2+}$$

The electrons transferred from the zinc metal to the copper ions in the displacement experiment cannot be used to do any useful work, such as lighting a bulb or driving a motor. However, if we separate the zinc and copper, as shown in Figure 6, we can make the electrons flow through a wire. The wire can be connected to a bulb or a motor and we can now use the energy from the displacement reaction.

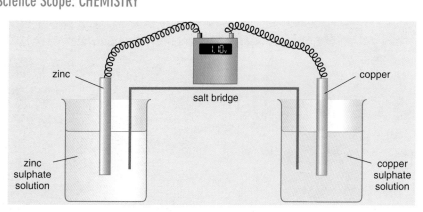

Figure 6 ▲

Extension box

The rechargeable battery

When the chemicals in a normal battery are used up, the battery has to be thrown away and replaced. This is because the chemical reactions that provided the electrical energy cannot be reversed.

The reactions in rechargeable batteries are reversible. The most common rechargeable battery is the nickel–cadmium (or Ni-Cad) battery. The battery consists of two pieces of steel mesh, one plated with cadmium, the other plated with nickel. The two pieces of plated mesh are separated by an absorbent plastic sheet soaked with potassium hydroxide solution, this does the same job as the acid in the simple cell we met earlier. The potassium hydroxide solution is called the electrolyte in the cell. A Ni-Cad battery gives a voltage of about 1.2 volts.

The reaction taking place while the battery is providing power (discharging) is:

cadmium + nickel(III) + water → cadmium + nickel(II)
         hydroxide   hydroxide   hydroxide

$$Cd + 2NiOOH + 2H_2O \rightarrow Cd(OH)_2 + 2Ni(OH)_2$$

The reaction above can be reversed by applying a voltage to the terminals of the cell from a battery charger:

cadmium + nickel(II) → cadmium + nickel(III) + water
         hydroxide   hydroxide   hydroxide

$$Cd(OH)_2 + 2Ni(OH)_2 \rightarrow Cd + 2NiOOH + 2H_2O$$

It is not enough to be able simply to reverse the reactions when the battery is charged, the battery must be capable of being recharged many times without any loss in performance.

Extension box continued

The light stick

It has been known for some time that certain insects, such as the firefly, can generate light chemically. The firefly makes light by reacting a substance called luciferin with an enzyme called luciferase. Enzymes are biological catalysts that work very efficiently; the firefly's method of making light is much better than anything scientists have devised yet. Over 80 % of the reacting luciferin molecules go on to give out light, compared to only 5–10 % in the scientists' experiments.

Being able to make light using chemicals would be really useful. Scientists decided to see if they could produce a light stick like this. They knew that they needed a substance like luciferin, that when given energy would give some of that energy out again as light. Any reactions like this are always the same:

$$A + B \rightarrow (I^*)$$

The substance I* is a molecule that has been given extra energy by the reaction between A and B. It is known as an *excited molecule*. I* then reacts with a coloured dye in the light stick to give it energy, some of this energy is given out as light. The dye gives out light by converting chemical energy to light, a process called **chemiluminescence**.

$$(I^*) + dye \rightarrow products + light$$

The trick is to come up with a reaction to produce an energetic molecule (I*) that has a lot of chemical energy, but is formed without too much heat being given out at the same time. Some of the chemicals used in the light stick are quite complicated.

Light sticks are used as safe light sources where sparks from an electric light might be a hazard. Or they can be used for lighting in an emergency. Light sticks are plastic tubes that contain a dye and a small glass container of another substance. When the light stick is bent, the glass container breaks and its contents mix with the dye, producing light.

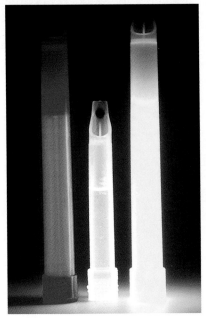

Figure 7 ▲ Light sticks

Types of chemical reaction

The many chemical reactions that are known about can be classified under various headings. The types considered here are:

- thermal decomposition
- synthesis
- oxidation
- reduction
- precipitation.

Thermal decomposition

Many substances are broken down into simpler substances when they are heated. For example, when copper carbonate is heated, it breaks down into copper oxide and carbon dioxide:

$$CuCO_3 \rightarrow CuO + CO_2$$

Breaking down a substance into simpler substances by heat is called **thermal decomposition**. The chemical change is obvious from the change in appearance of the reactant and products.

The thermal decomposition of calcium carbonate is an important reaction used in the building industry. Quicklime, chemical name calcium oxide, is made in this process, as shown in the word equation below:

$$\text{calcium carbonate} \xrightarrow{\text{heat}} \text{calcium oxide} + \text{carbon dioxide}$$
$$\text{(quicklime)}$$
$$CaCO_3(s) \rightarrow CaO(s) + CO_2(g)$$

The calcium oxide is then heated with clay to form cement. Cement is an ingredient of concrete, an important building material.

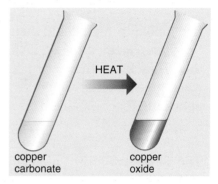

Figure 8 ▲ Copper carbonate decomposes when heated

Synthesis

Thermal decomposition makes new substances by breaking down a substance into simpler ones. **Chemical synthesis** is the exact opposite of this; more complex substances are made from simpler ones.

One of the most important examples of chemical synthesis is **photosynthesis**. In photosynthesis green plants use the Sun's energy to convert carbon dioxide and water into carbohydrates. The plants then use the carbohydrates to make their leaves and stems.

$$6CO_2 + 6H_2O \rightarrow C_6H_{12}O_6$$
$$\text{glucose}$$

Elements are the simplest substances known and contain only one type of atom. When elements react, more complex substances are always formed. An example of this is the synthesis of ammonia from hydrogen and nitrogen. The ammonia is then used to make fertilisers.

Nitrogen is essential for healthy plant growth and was traditionally supplied as manure from animals. Early in the twentieth century the population was increasing rapidly and there were fewer farm animals to provide manure. It became essential to find a way to make nitrogen from the air into ammonia. Fritz Haber (1868–1934) devised a way to make ammonia from nitrogen and hydrogen, using an iron catalyst. He was awarded the 1918 Nobel Prize for Chemistry for his work.

$$N_2 + 3H_2 \rightarrow 2NH_3$$
ammonia

Oxidation

Figure 9 ▲

Many substances change their appearance when heated in air, or when left in contact with air for a long time without heating. These changes suggest that chemical reactions have taken place. The substances are reacting with the oxygen in the air to form new substances, called oxides. These kinds of reactions are called **oxidation** reactions.

A good example of an oxidation reaction is the rusting of iron, which you will have seen on any old car, see Figure 9. The metal of the car reacts with the oxygen in the air to form a flaky red-brown substance that we call rust. The chemical name for rust is iron oxide.

The results of the experiments shown in Figure 10 indicate that iron will not rust unless air (oxygen) and water are both present.

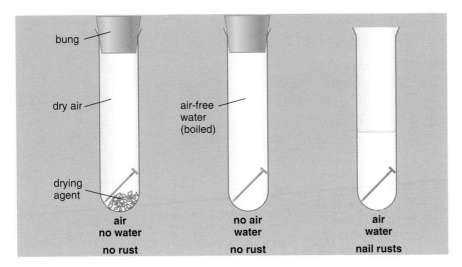

Figure 10 ▲

The combustion of fuels

The burning of methane, the gas used in Bunsen burners, is also an example of oxidation. When methane burns, each of the atoms present joins to oxygen atoms.

methane + oxygen $\rightarrow$ carbon dioxide + water

$$CH_4 + 2O_2 \rightarrow CO_2 + 2H_2O$$

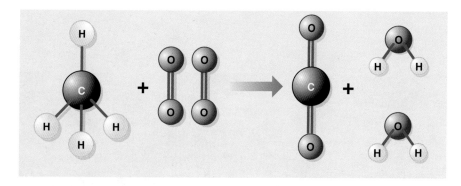

Figure 11 ◀

The combustion of fuels such as methane provides the energy modern society needs for manufacturing, transport and electricity, and so does much to make our lives comfortable.

Reduction

Reduction is the reverse of oxidation. Substances are reduced when oxygen is removed from them. Chemicals that remove oxygen from other substances are called **reducing agents**.

When black copper oxide is heated in a stream of hydrogen, it is reduced to pink copper metal. Droplets of water are also formed in the apparatus, shown in Figure 12. In this reaction, hydrogen has taken the oxygen away from the copper oxide and so hydrogen is the reducing agent. The hydrogen reacts with the oxygen to form water that is visible on the apparatus. Hydrogen is a good reducing agent because water, the compound it forms with oxygen, is very stable. This reaction can be summarised by the following equations:

copper oxide + hydrogen $\rightarrow$ copper + water

$$CuO + H_2 \rightarrow Cu + H_2O$$

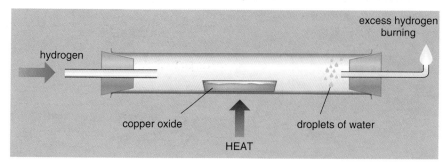

Figure 12 ▲

An important reduction reaction is used in the manufacture of iron. In this case, carbon is the reducing agent. Carbon is added to a blast furnace in the form of coke, and reduces iron oxide to iron in the following reaction:

$$\text{iron oxide} + \text{carbon} \rightarrow \text{carbon dioxide} + \text{iron}$$
$$2Fe_2O_3 + 3C \rightarrow 3CO_2 + 4Fe$$

Carbon dioxide, like water, is also a very stable substance.

Precipitation

We saw earlier that the test for carbon dioxide was the formation of a precipitate when carbon dioxide is passed into limewater (Chapter 2, page 19). Sometimes when two solutions are mixed they react to form a precipitate.

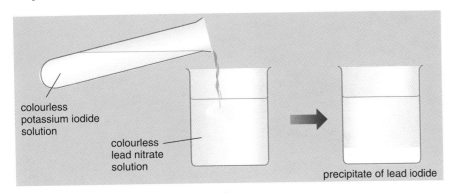

colourless potassium iodide solution

colourless lead nitrate solution

precipitate of lead iodide

Figure 14 ▲ A precipitation reaction

Figure 13 ▲ A blast furnace

raw materials in:
iron ore
coke
limestone

waste gases out

waste gases out

blast zone

air in

air in

slag out

iron out

Because precipitates are easy to see, many reactions in which precipitates form are used as chemical tests. A **test** is a reaction that works for only one substance or type of substance. For example, the test for carbon dioxide only works with carbon dioxide – we can use the test to tell it apart from any other gas.

In a precipitation test, the substance to be tested is mixed with a test solution and if a precipitate forms the test is positive. Table 3 describes the tests for chlorides, sulphates and lead compounds.

Test solution	Substance detected	Positive result
silver nitrate	chlorides, e.g. sodium chloride	white precipitate
barium chloride	sulphates, e.g. zinc sulphate	white precipitate
potassium iodide	lead compounds, e.g. lead nitrate	yellow precipitate

Table 3 ▲

The law of conservation of mass

When chemical reactions take place, the atoms in the reactants are rearranged to form different substances – called the products.

The burning of methane is an example. The reaction can be represented by the equation:

$$CH_4 + 2O_2 \rightarrow CO_2 + 2H_2O$$

We can imagine the molecules of methane and oxygen being broken up into separate atoms. We can then imagine these atoms recombining to form the products, carbon dioxide and water.

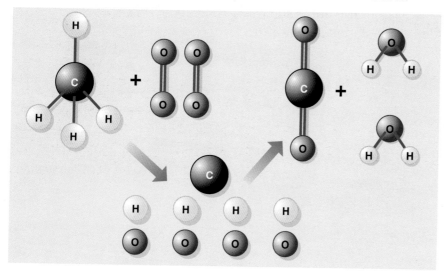

Figure 15 ◀

Notice that the total number of atoms remains the same in the reactants and the products. Since the masses of the carbon atoms, the oxygen atoms and the hydrogen atoms do not change, the mass of the products must be the same as the mass of the reactants.

This observation holds good for all reactions and it is summarised in the law of conservation of mass:

> **In a chemical reaction mass is conserved.**

Figure 14 also makes the point that during a chemical reaction atoms combine in different ways, but are neither created nor destroyed in the reaction.

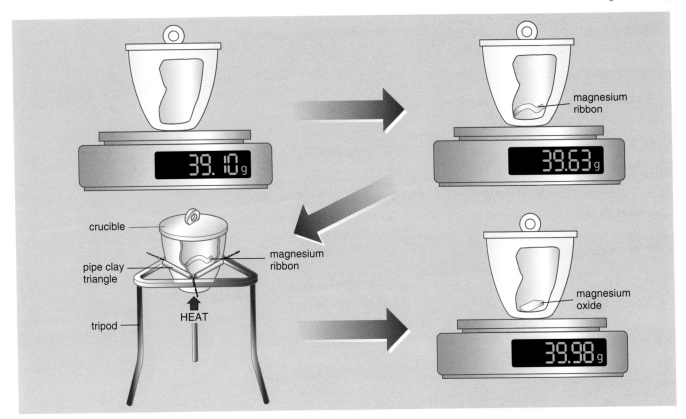

Figure 16 ▲ Magnesium increases in mass when it reacts with oxygen

Reactions involving gases

Magnesium burns in air to form magnesium oxide:

$$2Mg + O_2 \rightarrow 2MgO$$

The mass of magnesium oxide formed is always greater than the mass of magnesium used. Oxygen is taken from the air and combines permanently with the magnesium. Mass has still been conserved; it is just that the amount of oxygen taken from the air cannot be measured. However, the amount of oxygen combined with the magnesium can be measured.

Table 4 shows the result of burning magnesium in air and weighing the magnesium oxide formed.

Mass of magnesium burned in g	Mass of oxide formed in g
0.56	0.94
0.80	1.34
1.10	1.84
1.32	2.19

Table 4 ▲

Test Yourself

8 How does the mass of magnesium oxide formed depend on the mass of magnesium burned?

9 What mass of magnesium oxide would be formed from 2.20 g of magnesium?

10 What mass of magnesium oxide would be formed from 0.40 g of magnesium?

11 Describe how you could work out what mass of magnesium oxide would be formed when 0.95 g of magnesium was burned. Now calculate the mass of magnesium oxide that would be formed.

Look at Figure 17. The first part shows the start of the reaction between copper carbonate and acid in a flask. The flask is on the pan of a balance. The second part shows the flask when the reaction has finished.

Figure 17 ◀

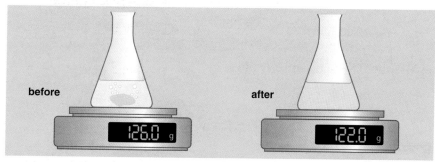

Mass appears to have been lost as the reaction proceeds, but only because the carbon dioxide formed escapes and no longer registers on the balance. If we could catch the carbon dioxide formed, the mass of the reactants and products would be the same.

Mass is also conserved when solutions form and when substances melt or boil.

Consider the reaction between carbon and oxygen:

$$C + O_2 \rightarrow CO_2$$

For every carbon atom reacted, a molecule of carbon dioxide is formed. If two carbon atoms were reacted, we would get two molecules of carbon dioxide and so on.

This reasoning is valid for all chemical reactions and leads to the general rule that:

> **The mass of the products formed is equal to the mass of the reactants used.**

Test Yourself

12 What mass of carbon dioxide was formed in the reaction shown in Figure 17?

Summary

When you have finished studying this chapter, you should understand that:

✔ Fossil fuels were formed millions of years ago from plant remains.

✔ Fossil fuels can be burnt to produce carbon dioxide, water and heat energy.

✔ Burning too much fossil fuels increases the greenhouse effect.

✔ Harmful acid rain is formed when the sulphur in fossil fuels is burnt.

✔ Electricity can be obtained from displacement reactions.

✔ Useful chemical reactions include thermal decomposition, synthesis, oxidation and reduction.

✔ During a chemical reaction, mass is conserved.

End-of-Chapter Questions

1   Explain in your own words the following key terms you have met in this chapter:

  fossil fuels

  hydrocarbon fuels

  incomplete combustion

  greenhouse effect

  acid rain

  catalytic converter

  thermal decomposition

  synthesis

  oxidation

  reduction

  reducing agent

2   Hydrogen might one day replace petrol as a fuel for cars. We could get the hydrogen by breaking down water into hydrogen and oxygen by passing an electric current through it, a process called electrolysis.

  a) Write a balanced equation, with state symbols, which shows water being broken down into hydrogen and oxygen.

  b) Why would it be a good thing to replace petrol as a fuel?

  c) Try to find out what advantages and disadvantages hydrogen has as a fuel, compared to petrol. Start at this web site: http://www.h2eco.org/

3   New buildings in large towns and cities often become coated with black grime.

  a) What pollutant is mainly responsible for the grime?

  b) Explain how this pollutant gets into the air.

4   A piece of iron wool was pushed into the end of a test tube and a few drops of water added to the iron wool. The test tube was inverted into a beaker of water and left, as shown below.

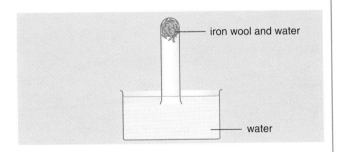

  iron wool and water

  water

After 2 days, the water had risen up the tube and the iron wool was covered with a brown powder.

  a) What is the common name and the chemical name for the brown powder?

  b) Explain why the water rose up the tube.

  c) Explain why the water didn't rise to fill the tube completely.

End-of-Chapter Questions continued

5 A teacher heated some calcium carbonate and it did not appear to change. The teacher said that thermal decomposition had occurred and new substances had been formed. John did not believe his teacher and said that the calcium carbonate could not have decomposed because it looked the same before and after heating.

   a) What does *thermal decomposition* mean?

   b) Explain why John was wrong when he said that the calcium carbonate could not have decomposed because there had been no change in its appearance.

   c) How could you prove to John that he was wrong? (There are two ways to do this, can you think of both of them?)

   d) Write a word equation for the thermal decomposition of calcium carbonate.

6 Fred heated up some shiny pieces of copper in an open test tube. The pieces of copper went black. Fred's teacher told him that the copper had been oxidised to form copper oxide.

   a) What is meant by *oxidised*?

   b) Write a word equation and a symbol equation for the oxidation reaction.

   c) Explain two ways in which Fred could make the copper shiny again.

7 Copper sulphate solution and sodium hydroxide solution react together to give a blue precipitate of copper hydroxide. The unbalanced equation for the reaction is:

$$CuSO_4 + NaOH \rightarrow Cu(OH)_2 + Na_2SO_4$$

   a) Balance the equation.

   b) Describe how you could use this reaction to show that it obeyed the Law of Conservation of Mass.

8 Each member of a class was given a test tube containing a different amount of copper carbonate to heat. They each weighed their tube and copper carbonate before heating it. They re-weighed the test-tube after heating it, once the tube had cooled down. They put their results together and drew a graph. Most of the class got results very near the line their teacher drew on the graph, but Lucy's result looked odd. It is shown on the graph.

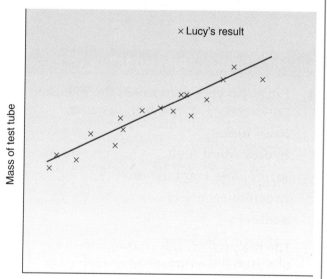

Mass of test tube and contents before heating

   a) How would you expect the appearance of the contents of the tube to change during heating?

   b) Name the two products of this reaction.

   c) How does the mass of the solid product depend on the mass of copper carbonate that was heated?

   d) Can you explain Lucy's odd result? How could she have prevented it?

   e) Explain why the mass of the test tube plus contents after heating is less than its mass before heating.

End-of-Chapter Questions continued

9 Five members of a class heated different amounts of magnesium in a weighed crucible, as shown below.

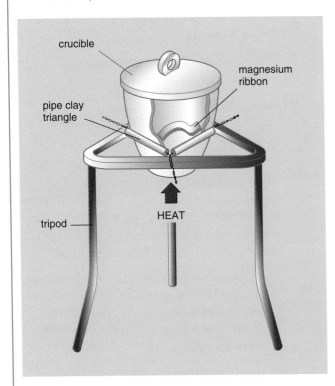

The magnesium was heated, lifting the lid of the crucible from time to time until no further reaction could be seen. The crucible was then allowed to cool and was re-weighed. The results are shown in the table.

b) Draw a graph of mass of magnesium (horizontal axis) against mass of magnesium oxide (vertical axis).

c) How does the mass of magnesium oxide formed depend on the mass of magnesium used?

d) What mass of magnesium oxide would be formed from 1.00 g of magnesium?

e) **i)** One of the results does not fit the general pattern. Which one is this?

ii) Suggest what might have led to this unusual result and indicate how it might have been avoided.

f) Why was the crucible lid lifted from time to time?

10 Which of the following types of reaction (there may be more than one) takes place in the reactions represented by the following equations.

thermal decomposition, synthesis, oxidation or reduction

a) $2Ca(NO_3)_2 \rightarrow 2CaO + 4NO_2 + O_2$

b) $N_2 + 3H_2 \rightarrow 2NH_3$

c) $CH_4 + 2O_2 \rightarrow CO_2 + 2H_2O$

d) $Fe_2O_3 + 3CO \rightarrow 2Fe + 3CO_2$

	John	Mary	Luke	Ralph	Fiona
Mass of crucible + lid in g	39.10	40.25	39.90	38.88	41.00
Mass of crucible + lid + magnesium in g	39.63	40.97	40.88	40.04	42.39
Mass of crucible + magnesium oxide + lid in g	39.98	41.45	41.54	40.63	43.32

a) Use the results in the table above to complete this table.

	John	Mary	Luke	Ralph	Fiona
Mass of magnesium in g					
Mass of magnesium oxide in g					

End-of-Chapter Questions continued

11 Joan and Andy set up the apparatus below to study the products of combustion from some liquid fuels. During an experiment to determine whether the products from a burning fuel included water and carbon dioxide, the following observations were recorded in their account.

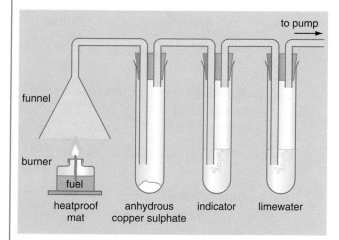

In the experiment, the funnel above the candle gradually became coated with a black substance and the anhydrous copper sulphate turned from white to blue. The indicator showed a pH of 6.0 and the limewater went milky. The amount of black substance formed on the funnel could be reduced by drawing air through the apparatus more quickly. If the tubes containing the indicator and limewater were interchanged it was very difficult to see any change at all in the indicator. However, interchanging the tubes containing the anhydrous copper sulphate and the indicator did not affect the results of the experiment.

a) Why was the burner placed on a heatproof mat?

b) i) Name the black substance which coated the funnel.

ii) Why was the black substance formed and why was less formed when the air flow was increased?

c) i) Was carbon dioxide formed? Explain your answer.

ii) Is carbon dioxide an acidic gas? Explain your answer.

d) Suggest why interchanging the tubes containing indicator and limewater affected the experimental results in the way stated.

e) What had Joan and Andy overlooked when they wrote that '. . . interchanging the tubes containing the anhydrous copper sulphate and indicator did not affect the results of the experiment'?

f) i) Supposing no chemicals that change colour with water had been available, what other test might have shown with reasonable certainty that water was formed?

ii) In such circumstances, what would you have done to the tube in which you intended to collect the water formed and why?

Andy did another experiment using the apparatus, but burnt a small piece of coal under the funnel. He noticed that the anhydrous copper sulphate changed very little compared with the liquid fuels they had used in other experiments. He also noticed that the indicator showed a pH of 4 in the experiment with coal.

g) i) Explain why the anhydrous copper sulphate changed less using coal than with a liquid fuel.

ii) How could you account for the lower pH in the experiment using coal?

Index

Note: page numbers in *italics* refer to illustrations

Photo Acknowledgements

The publishers would like to thank the following individuals, institutions and companies for permission to reproduce photographs in this book. Every effort has been made to trace ownership of copyright. The publishers would be happy to make arrangements with any copyright holder whom it has not been possible to contact:

Action Plus (8, 57); Andrew Lambert (32, 55 top three and bottom left and right, 56 middle, 131 bottom three, 132 both, 134 both); Author (75); British Museum (130 all); Collections/Graham Peacock (82 right); Corbis (16, 20 both, 47 bottom, 55 bottom middle, 87 left, 90, 100, 115 top left and bottom middle, 116, 138, 141 bottom, 148 top, 169, 175); GSF Picture Library (82 left, 83 all, 84 both, 86, 89 both, 91 both, 92, 95 both, 101, 103 both, 104 both, 105 all, 106 both, 109 all, 145 top left); Hodder & Stoughton (153); Holt (145 bottom left and right, 147); Life File (29, 31, 56 bottom right, 74, 115 top middle and right and bottom right, 141 top, 149 both); Natural History Museum (97 bottom); QA Photos (136); Salt Union (47 top left); Science Photo Library (28, 34, 56 top right, 87 right, 88, 94, 97 top and middle, 102, 115 bottom left, 119, 124, 129, 131 top, 154, 173); Topham Picturepoint (47 top right).

Figure 4, page 148 reproduced by kind permission of the Chapter of Wells.

Orders: please contact Bookpoint Ltd, 130 Milton Park, Abingdon, Oxon OX14 4SB. Telephone: (44) 01235 827720, Fax: (44) 01235 400454. Lines are open from 9.00 – 6.00, Monday to Saturday, with a 24 hour message answering service.
You can also order through our website www.hodderheadline.co.uk
British Library Cataloguing in Publication Data
A catalogue record for this title is available from The British Library
ISBN 0 340 80477 7

First published 2002
Impression number 10 9 8 7 6 5 4 3 2
Year   2008 2007 2006 2005 2004 2003

Cover photo from Science Photo Library.
Typeset by Fakenham Photosetting Ltd.
Printed in Italy for Hodder & Stoughton Educational, a division of Hodder Headline, 338 Euston Road, London NW1 3BH.